W9-CTF-213

a Year in Cookies

Naomi Spinak

Emissary
PRESS

Author's Note: *By all means, copy these recipes and give them to your friends. Please bake them and send them to someone who could use the love. But if you love the book so much you want to copy all the pages, just buy a new one. The money all goes to fund cancer research for kids, after all.*

A publication of
Emissary Press
PO Box 2222
Poulsbo, WA 98370

Illustrations and recipes © 2012 by Naomi Spinak.
All rights reserved. Published 2012.
Printed in the United States of America.
16 15 14 13 12   1 2 3 4 5

ISBN (paperback) 978-1-936672-42-4
Library of Congress Control Number 2012950574

Books distributed to the trade by
Seattle Book Company
www.seattlebookcompany.com

Cover design by Sheila Cowley

This book is dedicated to Logan Wight,
his family, and to all the other families touched
by children's cancer. May it help, even a little,
towards a cure.

It is also dedicated to Bess Katz, who was
especially fond of cookies and chocolate, and
who would get up in the middle of the night to
eat ice cream if someone invited her.

Contents

SPRING

SUMMER

Acknowledgments

Special thanks to all my recipe testers and editors: Ari Katz, Cestjon McFarland, Courtney Tate, Deb Rudnick, Elaine Sohn, Erin Cyger, Julie Cooper, Kendra Greathouse, Lane Lindberg, Laura Cannon, Lena Kim, Marissa Wachter, Phyllis Katz, Sara Hellold, Shaine McMahon, Sharon Katz Cooper, Ximena McIntosh and Sue Arkans, and to Courtney Tate for child wrangling.

An especially special thanks to Jessica Dubey and Kiran Spees for all their technical support with the book layout.

Another thanks to my husband, David, and children, Jacob and Mirit, for all their extensive testing and quality control, as well as all their other support.

And a BIG Thank You to donors, including: Deb Rudnick, Elaine Sohn, Janet Levi Pauli, Kelly Bethke, Sharon Katz Cooper, and Victor and Phyllis Katz.

A Year in Cookies

In August 2010 I found out from a middle school friend of mine that her four-year-old son had been diagnosed with brain cancer. It's a devastating diagnosis for anyone—but for a four-year-old?! How could any mother handle this? I had a four-year-old at the time, and I could not imagine what she was going through. She also had two other children and was pregnant with number four. A lot on her plate.

Although our friendship had faded with distance (I live on Bainbridge Island, outside Seattle, and she lives in Pleasanton, California, near Oakland), I still felt the connection we'd formed as part of a very close-knit group of girls in middle school. What could I do to help?

I have what some would call an addiction to baking. I decided to channel that addiction and send a little cheer her way, even if I couldn't do much else. I would force myself to make a goal and dedicate myself to keeping it: one batch of cookies every week for a year. I have to add that part of the idea came from a deck of cookie cards (The Cookie Deck) that I had just purchased at Powell's Books in Portland, which offered 52 recipes for cookies. My plan seemed a small thing, but maybe it could lead to bigger things. And maybe sending a little cheer and giving her something to look forward to in her life wouldn't be such a bad idea.

Then I started posting the cookies to my Facebook page. Then I got comments about the cookies and requests for recipes—a lot of comments and requests. I altered and substituted so much, I decided to write (and illustrate) this book and donate all the proceeds to kids' cancer research.

So, here it is, a cookie recipe each week for a year. 52 recipes. So maybe now I can send a little more cheer to a lot more people. And maybe some more progress can be made towards treating and curing juvenile brain tumors.

Naomi's Notes

ABOUT THE ILLUSTRATIONS

My real background (other than as a serious baking addict) is in art and costume design. I have always been a lover of fabric, with a love established firmly after years of tracking my mother around G Street Fabrics in Bethesda, MD (which is no longer there, by the way). My mother trained me to appreciate textures and colors, and I discovered that I love to "paint" with fabrics—and it's a lot less messy. The illustrations in this book are all "fabric collage." I pieced, glued, and stitched each piece by machine.

Ximena McIntosh then photographed the collages, and I then tweaked and fiddled with them in Photoshop. The original fabric pieces will go into a quilt that will also be sold to benefit pediatric brain cancer research. The fabrics came from all over the world, from my mother's collection, and from my local fabric store, but most came from my "stash." I hope you will appreciate them as you bake for someone special.

PACKAGE CARE

Because all of the cookies had to go through the mail, I had to choose recipes that were good travelers. I generally stayed away from meringues, or ice-cream sandwiches or cream puffs. I suggest you make the cookies in this book to mail as well. As I have two small children, we always kept a few for us, so my kids wouldn't start to hate this far-off child for always taking their cookies! Be careful, though: some of the recipes didn't actually travel so well. So either get to know your mailing store very well, pack better than I did, or choose very carefully which ones to mail.

HEALTHY SUBSTITUTIONS

Partway through this journey, Sherry's new baby began having trouble with dairy. So all of these recipes can be made dairy-free, and I've noted that option. The only completely dairy- and soy-free margarine I've found is Earth Balance.

Since I have kids and a sweet tooth myself—did you guess?—I have recently experimented with whole wheat and low-sugar options while baking. I have found that the cookies are just as good, and unless you are completely addicted to sugar, many of them actually taste better because you can taste the other ingredients. Plus, I'm trying to start a revolution weaning us off refined white flour. Join in! Still, I wouldn't call this a health-food book!

Also, you could probably make quite a few of the cookies gluten-free as well, were you so inclined, by substituting rice and millet, and sometimes almond flour for the all-purpose or whole wheat flour. Try it out. Let me know.

INGREDIENTS

I have heard smart people say, "Cooking is an art, but baking is a science." I disagree. I have experimented with all of these recipes, and they have almost always turned out fine. Maybe they take a little finessing, but they have still been tasty. So go ahead, dive in! Don't be afraid to tinker.

Fancy cookbooks will tell you that the best ingredients available will yield the best results. They are right. However, busy moms will tell you that cookies are still yummy even if you are digging out last year's Halloween chocolate to get the right amount. I make suggestions in here for ingredients, but if you go with what you have or what's easy to get, I bet they will be fine. I am not a careful measurer, and I am usually baking with kid "help"—things still turn out fine.

I will say that eggs work better in these recipes at room temperature unless otherwise noted (you can always get them warmer quickly in a warm-water bath). I don't sift my flour. I also use brown sugar without checking if it is dark or light, and the same with molasses. Each one will give your cookies a slightly different flavor, but they're all good. Go with your favorite.

If butter is listed as softened, that is to make it easier to cream with the other ingredients. If you didn't leave it out on the counter for a while, you can microwave it for a few seconds. Otherwise, you will get lots of butter chunks instead of a smooth dough. But don't microwave it all the way to melted or the consistency will be too thin.

I try to use the best chocolate I can get, because I love chocolate. I like Scharffen Berger baking chocolate, which comes in different percentages, from unsweetened to milk chocolate. I usually use the 70 percent for a semisweet chocolate.

I list a number for the amount of cookies you will get, but I give no guarantees because they vary so much depending on how big you like your cookies. I usually get fewer cookies than a recipe says because I make my cookies big. MOST of these recipes make two standard-size baker's cookie sheets worth. Is that a good-enough estimate?

TOOLS

The good thing about cookies is that they generally don't need a lot of fancy baking equipment to make.

I have a set of three heavy-duty baking sheets from Costco and Silpat silicone liners that I think work very well. I also have a rack for cooling cookies. I have a stand mixer and a hand mixer, but you don't necessarily need both. I find my hand mixer is better for whipping egg whites (and it is very easy for my four-year-old to use). I occasionally use a food processor for mixing crumbly dough.

I have several good mixing bowls in different sizes and a sturdy rolling pin for roll-and-cut cookies. I used to have a marble one, but that was more useful for scaring off intruders than actually rolling dough. Now I have a "French" (Do they know baking best? I'd argue that the Italians are better. But nobody has a cookie tradition like the United States!) rolling pin, which is great because it's wooden (not super heavy) and one piece—no little interior bits to clean.

For some specialized cookies, I bought a cookie press (a hand press) and a madeleine pan.

It is also fun to have a variety of cookie cutters for roll-out cookies. My set keeps growing as I get inspired and as my children's interests appear. I have an alphabet and number set (to make learning sweet!), a Chanukah set (which mysteriously includes something that looks like a Christmas tree; we think it's supposed to be a menorah), an airplane, a helicopter that usually breaks in the making because a piece is too thin, a dachshund (that's my brother's fault), a set of snowflakes (because they were too pretty), a set of hearts, some fall leaves, and a new Cars set because my son is obsessed. I think you can get a cookie cutter for just about any interest you have. I once wandered into a shop in Seattle that was almost entirely cookie cutters. Strangely enough, I have no circle cookie cutters. I just use different glasses to get different sizes. Depending on space, you may just want to cut your cookies with a small knife (or go with the glasses) and not start a collection. I think mine is getting a little out of control.

Okay, maybe there's more equipment than I thought. Still, if you're not making every cookie in the book, you can get away with a lot less. Not that I'd suggest that.

All of the temperature instructions are in Fahrenheit.

FINALLY

I can't believe a whole year (of cookies) passed by so quickly. Logan was doing okay when I finished sending the cookies. He got out of the hospital and got to spend some time with his family. Unfortunately, while I was working on this book, the medications and disease took their toll on his little body. Logan Wight passed away February 11, 2012. He was five and a half. I hope that this book is a tribute to him and to his fun-loving spirit and his family. I hope we can look back and say we helped to make a difference for other families, even if we can't help Logan now. We will remember him, though, every time we make cookies.

The process of making and promoting this book also taught me a lot about the power of small gestures. From a Kickstarter campaign that so many friends supported and passed on, to word-of-mouth in my own community and the will-ingness of small businesses to help, I've seen that big things can grow from one little idea. You're reading this now, so thanks for being a part of it too.

People really do care, and this project is a great example of that spirit.

Triple Chocolate Drop Cookies

WHERE TO START? My year began in September. Leaves were turning, school had started, the Jewish High Holidays were looming, and Logan was diagnosed with cancer. I started with what I knew. Chocolate. Lots of it. What do you think of when you think of sending a box of cookies? If you're me, it's chocolate chip cookies.

INGREDIENTS

1/2 cup vegetable shortening (I use an all canola oil version)

1/2 cup butter or dairy-free, soy-free margarine (Earth Balance) softened

1/2 cup sugar (or evaporated cane juice if you are from the Northwest)

1/4 cup brown sugar

1 tsp baking soda

2 eggs (from volunteer chickens)

1 tsp vanilla extract

2 oz. unsweetened baking chocolate (fair trade, please), melted

1/4 cup unsweetened cocoa powder (I used Dagoba)

1 cup all-purpose flour, unbleached, as local as you can find it

1 cup whole wheat flour, as above

10 oz. white chocolate baking chunks or chips

TO MAKE THE COOKIES

Preheat the oven to 375 degrees. Line 2 cookie sheets with liners.

In a large mixing bowl, beat the shortening and buttery fat on medium to high speed in a mixer until fluffy. Add both kinds of sugar and the baking soda, beat until combined. Beat in the eggs, vanilla, and melted chocolate. Beat in the cocoa powder and finally the flour. Stir in the white chocolate chips.

Try not to eat too much of the dough as you drop tablespoons of dough onto cookie sheets. I use silicone baking liners, but parchment will work as well. Bake about 10–15 minutes, until tops are dry.

Cool on wire racks, if you eat them right out of the oven, the melted chocolate will burn your tongue.

Makes around 3 dozen.

Checkerboards

THESE ARE REALLY FUN roll, slice, and bake cookies. Again, chocolate won the day. The ones on the end will not be as pretty as the middle, but if you're the one to eat them no one has to know.

INGREDIENTS

1 cup butter or Earth Balance margarine, softened

1/4 cup sugar

1/4 cup brown sugar

1 1/2 tsp baking powder

1 egg

2 tsp vanilla extract

2 cups whole wheat flour

1 1/4 cups all purpose flour

2 oz. unsweetened chocolate, melted and cooled in a medium bowl

TO MAKE THE COOKIES

In a large mixing bowl, beat the butter with a mixer until fluffy. Add both sugars and baking powder, beat until combined. Beat in the egg and vanilla. Beat in the flour. Divide the dough in half.

Put half the dough in the bowl with the melted chocolate and knead the chocolate in until combined. This would be an ideal step for your eager young child. Then wipe down the counters, floor, hands, and fridge. Not in that order. Go start a load of laundry. Continue.

Shape each half of the dough into a log about 9 inches long. (Start with vanilla log, or both will be chocolate). Wrap each log in waxed paper or plastic wrap or your favorite reusable wrapping material. Chill for about 2 hours, or until after (the kids') bedtime. Cut each log lengthwise into quarters, and reassemble into two logs with alternating quarters as follows: Lay down a chocolate quarter. Put a vanilla quarter next to it. Put a vanilla quarter on top of the chocolate quarter, and a chocolate quarter next to that one on top of the first vanilla quarter. Look at the cross-section from the end and you should have a checkerboard (like the illustration) Roll the log on a board a bit to make them all stick together. Repeat with the other quarters. Wrap again and chill for another half an hour.

Preheat the oven to 375 degrees. Line two cookies sheets with silicone liners or parchment.

Slice the logs into quarter inch slices and place 2 inches apart on cookie sheets. Bake about 10 minutes or until bottoms are lightly browned.

Remove and cool on a rack.

Makes about 20 small cookies, give or take the ends.

Pecan Florentines

THESE COOKIES WERE ALWAYS MY FAVORITE at the bakery near our house, especially when dipped in chocolate. I never made them before this week though, and I found out why. They're kind of a pain. And, they take up lots of space and may completely stick to the tray. When I say grease the tray, I mean it. Although my cousin Sue had no trouble with ungreased parchment. I can't explain it. Also, you could single-handedly eat the whole batch in about 10 minutes because they are thin. If I were you, I would go ahead and double the recipe. Don't say I didn't warn you.

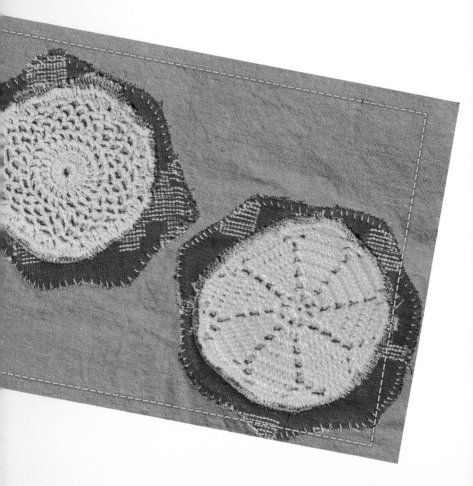

INGREDIENTS

1/4 cup sugar

1/3 cup melted butter or Earth Balance

2 tsp molasses

1 Tbsp milk, soy milk, almond milk, or coconut milk. Pick your poison.

1/2 cup ground pecans. You can also use walnuts, but then you have to call them Walnut Florentines.

1/4 cup all purpose flour

2 oz. bittersweet chocolate, chopped (optional)

TO MAKE THE COOKIES

Preheat the oven to 325 degrees.

Line cookie sheets with foil and grease the foil. I mean it. You could also try greased parchment, but really, do use cooking spray, butter, oil, something so you can eventually remove the cookies from the tray in a manner that will enable you to eat or serve whole cookies. DON'T USE A SILICONE MAT, THE COOKIES MAY NEVER SET.

In a medium mixing bowl, stir together the sugar, melted butter, molasses, and milk. Stir in the ground nuts and flour.

Drop teaspoons of the batter 3 or 4 inches apart on the cookie sheet. They will spread a lot, so maybe 6 per sheet. Bake until bubbly and browned, 8–10 minutes. Then turn off the oven and leave the cookies in for another 10 minutes. Remove from the oven and put the whole parchment sheet on a rack to cool. If you are going to mail them, you will want waxed paper between each cookie.

If desired, melt the chocolate in the microwave, in short bursts, first 30 seconds, then stir to test and repeat 15 seconds at a time until melted and smooth. Drizzle over cookies or dip cookies in. Let dry on rack.

Makes about 10 large cookies.

Honey Cardamom Cut Outs

THESE HAVE A SOMEWHAT PERSIAN FLAVOR to me, because of the cardamom. They are quite different from your average sugar cookie. Bake whatever shapes you prefer.

INGREDIENTS

1/2 cup butter or Earth Balance

1/4 to 1/2 cup brown sugar
depending on preferred sweetness or leave out completely.

1 tsp baking powder

1/2 tsp ground cardamom

1 egg

1/2 cup honey

2 cups whole wheat flour

1 cup all purpose flour

TO MAKE THE COOKIES

Beat the butter with an electric mixer until soft and fluffy. Add the sugar, baking powder, and cardamom and beat until combined. Beat in the egg and the honey, and then the flour. Divide in half, wrap, press into discs, and chill until easy to roll: 3 hours to overnight.

Preheat the oven to 375 degrees. Grease 2 cookie trays or line with parchment or silicone liners.

On a lightly floured surface, roll each half of the dough to a 1/4 inch thickness. Cut out shapes, repeat with all dough.

Bake until lightly browned on edges: 9 minutes or whatever your oven does in that vicinity. Remove and cool on a rack. Decorate with icing if you like.

Makes 3 dozen or so, depending on cookie size and shape.

Lemon–Pistachio Pretzels

THESE ARE REALLY FUN TO MAKE WITH A SMALL CHILD. You can also make them into letters, or other fun shapes. Just make sure not to handle them so much that you won't want to eat them.

INGREDIENTS

3/4 cup butter or Earth Balance, softened

1 cup confectioner's sugar

2 tsp finely shredded lemon zest —I have a nifty zester, saves you bloody fingers

1 egg

1/2 tsp lemon extract or lemon oil

1 cup whole wheat flour

1 cup white flour

GLAZE:

1 Tbsp freshly squeezed (yeah, right) **or bottled lemon juice.** Believe me, it's not worth the effort.

1/2 cup confectioner's sugar

1 to 2 Tbsp water

1/3 cup finely chopped pistachio nuts (salted or unsalted)

TO MAKE THE COOKIES

Beat the butter with a mixer until fluffy and soft. Like a puppy. OK, maybe not. You just want it to be able to combine with the other ingredients without lumps. Beat in one cup of the sugar and the zest. Beat in the egg and the lemon extract or oil. Beat in the flour. Divide dough in half, wrap, and flatten into discs. Chill for at least 30 minutes, or 1 episode of *Glee*.

Preheat the oven to 375 degrees. Line 2 cookie sheets with your choice of liner.

On a floured pastry board or rolling board or whatever you call the space where you roll cookies or knead bread were you to do such a thing, shape each half into a log. Cut each log into 24 pieces. Approximately. You could also make more bigger pretzels. These come out quite small. Anyway, roll each piece into a snake, and shape into a pretzel, a snake, a Greek spiral, or your desired shape.

Place on cookie sheets, leaving a little space for spreading. There's only one egg for rising, so don't expect too much expansion. Hey, if you want exact instructions, you should read Julia Child.

Bake until golden brown, 10 minutes in my oven. Start checking at 8. Remove from cookie sheet and cool on a rack.

GLAZE

In a small bowl, stir together the glaze ingredients, adding water as needed to make smooth. Brush it on with a pastry brush (I like my silicone one because it doesn't leave little hairs in the cookies). Sprinkle with the chopped pistachios. Yes, your counter will get messy because I just said the cookies were on a rack, and then I had you glaze them and add nuts. So have your child lick the counter, or wipe it up. Let the cookies stand until the glaze is set.

Makes 2 cookie sheets' worth.

Freaky Fingers

THANKS TO EPICURIOUS.COM for the inspiration for these cookies. Also, thanks to my son for picking them out. We were now up to Halloween in the cookie year, which happened to approximately follow the Jewish calendar, coincidentally. It wouldn't have been exactly that, but my oven broke around week 2 and I had to wait a while to bake again. It made for quite the creative Jewish New Year baking, let me tell you. Was it a sign?

I digress. Anyway, these are for Halloween, or whenever the need to eat fingers strikes you.

INGREDIENTS

1 cup butter or Earth Balance, softened

1/2 cup powdered sugar

1 egg

1 tsp vanilla extract

1 3/4 cup whole wheat flour

1 cup all purpose flour

1 tsp baking powder

1 tsp salt

"GLUE:"

A few Tablespoons powdered sugar

A few drops water If you are a four-year-old boy (or girl, I'm not being gender biased) you may demand to add a drop of red food coloring for a bloody effect. If you are opposed to artificial coloring, you may substitute cherry juice if you like. Make sure it is organic and local. Luckily, we live in the Northwest, so they are local, but not at Halloween time. We do have frozen cherries though. Make sure they are Bing and not Rainier, which will not actually give you a red color. Or skip the color.

Sliced almonds, as many as you have fingers (finger cookies that is)

TO MAKE THE COOKIES

In a large mixing bowl, beat the butter or margarine until smooth and creamy. Add the sugar, egg, and vanilla until combined. Add the flour, baking powder, and salt and beat until all mixed. If you have the Cookie Doodle app, **www.shoethegoose.com/CookieDoodle.aspx** you know what mixed looks like.

Wrap the dough or store in a closed container for an hour or until after bedtime.

Preheat the oven to 325 degrees. Line 2 cookie sheets with liners.

Divide the dough into 50 pieces. Alternatively, take about a tablespoon and roll into a finger shape, sort of a cylinder. If the dough gets too sticky, put back in the fridge, or flour your hands a little. Place the fingers (don't you feel a little like Frankenstein?) about 3 inches apart on the cookie sheet. Use a butter knife (we have little IKEA kid knives, which are perfect; a spreader will work as well) to create knuckle marks. Flatten one end of each cookie to have a place for the nail.

Bake 25 minutes or until slightly golden brown. Let cool. Mix together the glue ingredients until smooth, and use a dab to place an almond fingernail on the flat end of each cookie. Let dry. Arrange in groups of five around your house for full effect.

Makes a few spare hands worth.

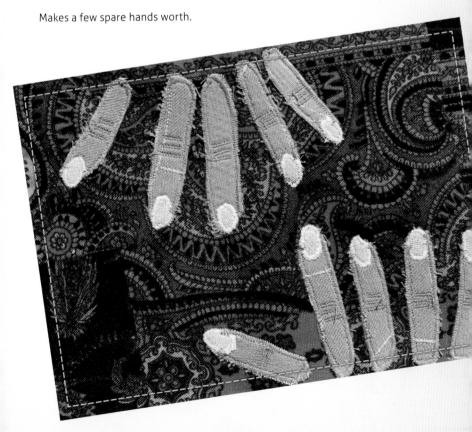

Blondies with Chocolate Chips

SO, I BAKED A LOT AROUND HALLOWEEN and wanted a quick recipe for this week that wasn't too fussy. Plus, a whole month without chocolate? That had to be stopped. My brother commented that blondies don't actually count as cookies but as usual, I ignored him. They can be eaten without a fork and they're sweet, so they're cookies.

INGREDIENTS

1 cup brown sugar

1/8 cup maple syrup

2/3 cup butter or Earth Balance

2 eggs

2 teaspoons vanilla extract

1 cup whole wheat flour

1 cup all purpose flour

1 teaspoon baking powder

1/2 teaspoon baking soda

1 cup semisweet or bittersweet chocolate (63 percent cocoa? 70 percent?), chopped, or Ghiradelli baking chunks. You may have to chop your own if you want it completely dairy free.

2/3 cup toasted almonds or hazelnuts (optional)

TO MAKE THE COOKIES

Preheat the oven to 350 degrees. Yay, a recipe you don't have to chill.

Grease a 13 by 9 by 2 inch baking pan. I won't tell anyone if you use a slightly different size. Just adjust the cooking time a little. Not that it's exact anyways.

In a LARGE saucepan over medium heat (on my stove this means the middle burner, the front ones will burn too fast), heat the sugar, maple syrup, and butter stirring constantly until the sugar dissolves. If you don't stir constantly, and you, for example, decide to go throw in a load of laundry, the mix will burn and you'll have to throw it out and start over. Don't chance it, just stir. Be zen about it.

Remove the pan from the heat and let cool slightly (that means you can go throw in that load of laundry now). Add the eggs one at a time.

If you are baking with a kid, now is the time to wash the raw egg off their fingers so they don't lick it. Mix with a wooden spoon until well blended. Stir in the vanilla. Stir in the flour, baking powder, and baking soda. Now you see why the saucepan was large. If you used a small one, you'll have to pour the whole thing into a big bowl and now you'll have two things to wash. And you have no one to blame but yourself.

Spread the batter into the prepared pan and sprinkle with chopped chocolate and nuts if so desired. We are not a brownie-with-nuts- loving family so we do not desire. But if you're different, we're cool with that.

Bake until done, about 35 minutes. Cut into bars, cool in pan.

Makes about 24 bars, depending on the size of your cuts.

Cinnamon Curls

MY SON MUST HAVE BEEN HOME from school, because this is another fussy week. Also, I may have switched the weeks around a bit, but I don't think that will affect the taste. Again, make whatever shapes you like best.

INGREDIENTS

3/4 cup butter or Earth Balance, softened: leave it on the counter while you eat breakfast

1/2 cup brown sugar. "They" always say packed, but I say measure how you like. If it's a little less, it won't matter. Uh, oh, now the sugar lobby is coming after me.

1 tsp cinnamon, or more if you can take it

1/4 tsp baking powder

1 egg

1 tsp vanilla extract

1 cup all-purpose flour (I use Stone Buhr; it's as local as I can get from the supermarket)

1 cup whole wheat flour

TOPPING:

1 Tbsp turbinado sugar or evaporated cane juice

1 egg white (or heck, throw in the whole egg if you don't want to waste), beaten slightly

1/2 tsp cinnamon

Mini chocolate chips (if you can find non dairy ones, you win a prize) or candy covered sunflower seeds or other small treats to decorate

TO MAKE THE COOKIES

In a large mixing bowl, beat the butter or butter substitute until smooth and creamy. Beat in brown sugar, 1 teaspoon cinnamon, and baking powder. Beat in the egg and vanilla. Beat in flour. Divide in half.

Preheat the oven to 375 degrees. Line or grease 2 cookie sheets.

In a small bowl, mix remaining cinnamon and turbinado sugar and set aside.

On a lightly floured surface (not your dog)—a flat, hair-free surface—divide dough into tablespoon size portions. Roll each into a snake and coil, snail-like. Place about 2 inches apart on the baking sheet. Brush with egg or egg white. Sprinkle with cinnamon sugar.

Add small candy or chocolate chips if desired.

Bake until lightly browned, about 8–10 minutes. Remove and cool on a rack. Makes about 2 dozen.

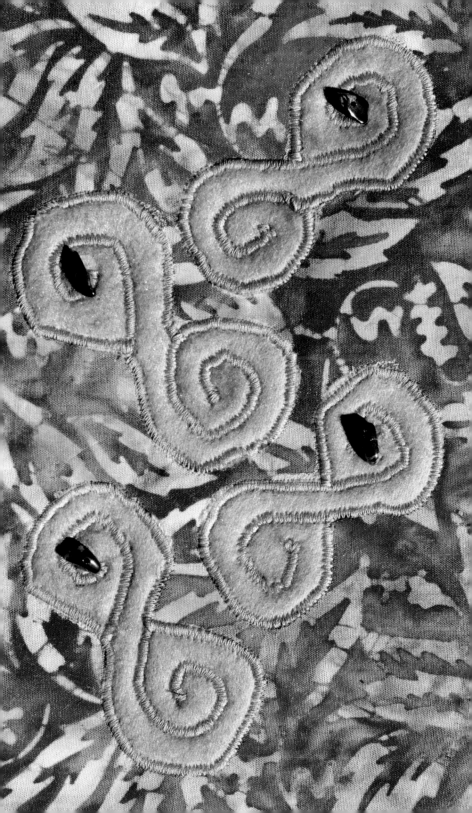

Pumpkin Squares with Crystallized Ginger

HERE COMES PUMPKIN TIME! These are a very cakey and not chewy bar. If you don't have crystallized ginger, you can throw in cinnamon or chocolate chips, or you can top with marshmallows or coconut. What do you like with pumpkin?

INGREDIENTS

1/2 cup all purpose flour

1 cup whole wheat flour

1/2 cup brown sugar

1/4 cup granulated sugar

2 tsp baking powder

1/4 tsp baking soda

1/4 to 1/3 cup finely chopped crystallized ginger (depending on how much you like ginger)(it is in the Asian foods section of my market. If you can't find it, add 1 teaspoon ground or chopped fresh ginger. It will taste a little different, but still good)

1 tsp ground cinnamon, or more

1/4 tsp salt

2 eggs

1 cup canned pumpkin

1/2 cup vegetable oil (dairy free has no substitutions this week —hurray!)

TO MAKE THE COOKIES

Spray a a 10 x 15 inch jelly roll pan or a 13 x 9 baking pan with non stick cooking spray, or grease with a little oil. We have organic oil sprays at my market, but you might not be so lucky. If you don't have the right pan, you can try two smaller pans, or make the bars slightly thicker. No one will complain if their bar is too big.

Preheat the oven to 350 degrees.

In a large mixing bowl, stir together the flour, sugars, baking powder, baking soda, ginger product, cinnamon, and salt. In another mixing bowl (sorry, this recipe has more washing), beat the eggs and stir in the pumpkin and oil. Add wet ingredients to dry ingredients and stir until combined. That wasn't so hard, was it?

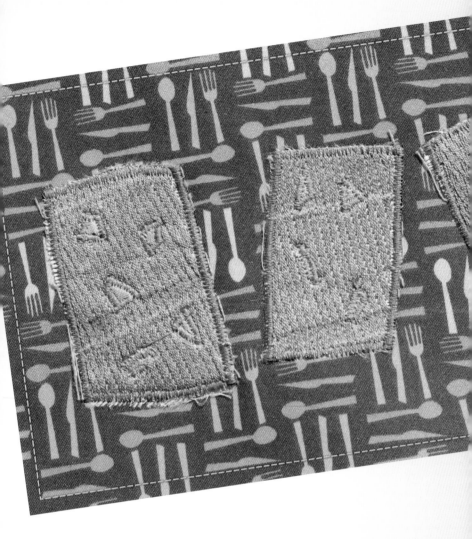

Spread the batter into the prepared pan. Bake until a toothpick comes out clean, about 20 minutes. Cool on a rack.

If you desire a topping (and who doesn't?), melt the chocolate in the microwave for about 15 seconds at a time with your solidified fat (the butter or margarine) until spreadable. Pipe stripes using a decorating bag or snipped plastic bag, or drizzle or spread on the bars. It's all up to you. Cut into squares.

Makes around 28 or so.

Molasses Ginger Crunch Cookies

You can probably tell we were getting into fall, my favorite time of year for baking, with pumpkin and all the fall spices. This week I happened to be in Maryland visiting my parents, but I didn't want to shirk my cookie-baking responsibilities. However, my parents are not as blessed with top quality supermarkets as we are on beautiful Bainbridge Island. This turned out to be a blessing in disguise. After two markets had no crystallized ginger, I bought Trader Joe's chocolate covered crystallized ginger. Inspiration!!! It ground up nicely in a small food processor and the cookies got dark chocolate AND ginger—not exactly a hardship. Still, I love my Town and Country Market.

INGREDIENTS

1 cup all purpose flour

1 cup whole wheat flour

2 1/2 tsp ground ginger

2 tsp baking soda

1 tsp ground cinnamon

1 teaspoon ground cloves

3/4 tsp salt

3/4 cup chopped crystallized ginger or one container of Trader Joe's dark chocolate covered crystallized ginger, pulverized

1/2 cup brown sugar

1/2 cup vegetable shortening, room temperature

1/4 cup unsalted butter or Earth Balance, softened

1 egg

1/4 cup molasses

1/2 cup turbinado or Sugar in the Raw for rolling cookies, maybe a little more

TO MAKE THE COOKIES

Combine flours, spices, and salt in a large bowl and stir to blend. Mix in crystallized ginger. Set aside. Using an electric mixer, beat brown sugar, shortening, and butter or butter substitute until fluffy. Add egg and molasses and beat until blended. Add dry ingredients and mix until combined. Remove from bowl, wrap in plastic wrap or your favorite non-disposable dough wrap, and chill for at least one hour in the fridge. If you chill longer, you may have to let the dough soften a little.

Preheat the oven to 350 degrees. Have two lined baking sheets ready, or grease your cookie sheets.

Put the turbinado sugar in a bowl. Form dough into 1 to 2 inch balls, and roll each ball in the sugar. You may need to wash your hands from time to time if they are getting too sticky, I know I did. Place the balls on the sheets about 2 inches apart. Bake until cracked on top and still slightly soft, 12–15 minutes. The bottoms will be dry. Cool slightly on sheets, and transfer to racks to dry.

Makes about 30 cookies.

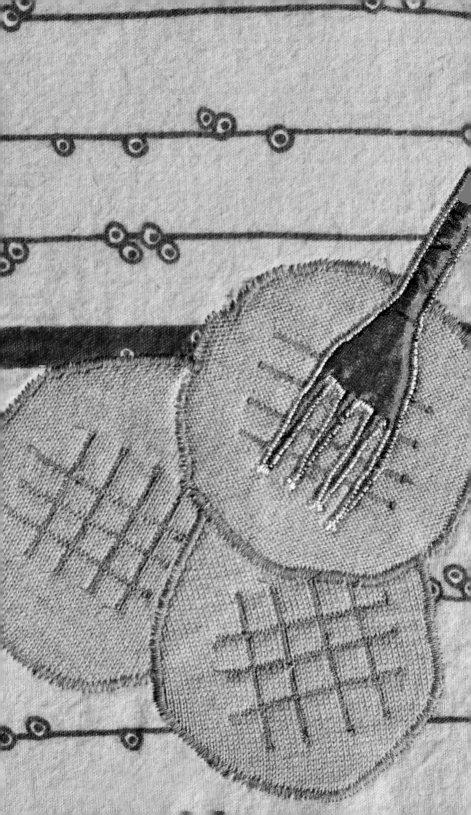

Peanut Butter Cookies

THIS WAS BEFORE THE PEANUT ALLERGY developed. But a cookie book couldn't be really complete without a good peanut butter cookie recipe. Just ask my sister. Anyway, in this one, the peanut butter is the fat. Only a small additional amount of butter. And check them soon, if you let them cook too long, they get dry.

INGREDIENTS

1 cup chunky peanut butter. I am not going to enter the debate (creamy vs. chunky). But I choose chunky because it's better.

1/4 cup butter or Earth Balance, softened

1/4 cup brown sugar

1/4 cup sugar or evaporated cane juice

1 egg

1/4 cup water
(or milk of some variety)

2 Tbsp maple syrup

1 tsp vanilla extract

1 tsp baking soda

1/2 tsp salt

1 3/4 cups whole wheat flour
or whole wheat pastry flour if you want them a little lighter

TO MAKE THE COOKIES

Preheat the oven to 350 degrees. Line 2 cookie sheets.

Cream the peanut butter, butter, sugars, egg, water, maple syrup, vanilla, baking soda, and salt in a medium bowl until blended. Add the flour until all combined into a stiff dough.

Drop by spoonfuls onto the baking sheets, 2 inches apart. Using a fork, make criss cross shapes on the cookies to flatten slightly. You may need to wet the fork several times to prevent sticking.

Bake the cookies until slightly browned, 10–13 minutes. Remove from oven and cool on racks.

Makes around 2 dozen.

Chocolate Mousse Cookies

NOW THESE WILL REALLY GIVE YOU YOUR CHOCOLATE FIX. They're like chocolate thumbprint cookies, but with something much better than Hershey's kisses for the filling! You can call me a chocolate snob; you just try it yourself and let me know.

INGREDIENTS

1/2 cup all purpose flour

3/4 cup whole wheat flour

1/2 tsp salt

1/2 tsp baking powder

1/4 tsp baking soda

1/2 cup unsalted butter or Earth Balance, softened

3/4 cup sugar or try even less

1/2 cup unsweetened cocoa powder (I use Dagoba)

3 eggs

3/4 tsp vanilla extract

3 oz. bittersweet or semisweet chocolate, melted and slightly cooled

FILLING:

3 oz. bittersweet chocolate, coarsely chopped

4 Tbsp unsalted butter or Earth Balance, cut into pieces

TO MAKE THE COOKIES

Preheat the oven to 350 degrees. Line cookie sheets with liners.

In a medium bowl, whisk the flour, salt, baking powder, and baking soda together.

In a stand mixer, beat the butter, sugar, and cocoa powder until well blended. Add the eggs one at a time, mixing until blended each time. Then add the vanilla. Blend another minute. Add the melted chocolate and blend. Add the flour and mix until well combined.

Drop tablespoonfuls of dough about 2 inches apart on the cookie sheets. Bake until the cookies are puffed and dry, 13–15 minutes. Use the back of a half teaspoon or your (clean) thumb to make indents in the cookies. Transfer to a rack to cool.

FILLING: Melt the chocolate and butter in the microwave, using 15 second increments and stirring until smooth.

Cool slightly and then spoon into the indents in the cookies, using a baby spoon or coffee spoon.

Set aside until the chocolate is firm, if you can, or eat immediately.

Makes about 3 dozen.

Chocolate Butter Spritz Cookies

AM I IN A CHOCOLATE PHASE? Doesn't bother me a bit. If you don't like it, skip ahead. I did buy a cookie press for these. I always wanted one anyway. It's a genetic habit. My Grandma Bess never met a kitchen gadget she didn't love. I have an awesome cake cutter/ server device from her, and a strawberry huller. She didn't pass a press on to me though!

If you need to make these dairy free, you can call them chocolate spritz, or Earth Spritz? Balance spritz? Maybe not. I didn't much lower the sugar on these because of the consistency needed for the press, so you may find them sweeter than some other cookies.

INGREDIENTS

1 cup unsalted butter or Earth Balance, softened

1/2 cup confectioner's sugar

1/2 cup brown sugar

1/4 cup unsweetened cocoa powder

1 egg yolk

2 Tbsp crème de cacao, milk, coconut milk or other chocolate flavoring (or other liquor I suppose. Why not go wild?)

1 Tbsp vanilla extract

1 cup all-purpose flour

1 1/3 cups whole wheat flour

Chocolate sprinkles or chopped nuts for topping, if desired

TO MAKE THE COOKIES

Preheat the oven to 375 degrees. Line 2 cookie sheets or leave plain.

Do not grease your sheets for these, or they won't release from the press.

In a large mixing bowl, cream the butter or Earth Balance until smooth. Add the sugars and cocoa powder and beat until combined. Beat in the egg yolk, flavoring of choice, and vanilla. Beat in the flour until all combined. You don't have to chill these, yay!

Pack the dough into your cookie press fitted with a pretty plate. My press was new, so I tried a lot of plates. My favorite made a sort of daisy shape. The ones with too many tiny holes just came apart.

Do read the instructions on your press so they come out nicely. On mine I had to press directly onto the ungreased sheets to get them to release. Place spritz cookies about 1 inch apart.

Decorate with nuts or sprinkles if you like.

Bake 10 minutes, or until firm. Remove and cool on a rack.

Makes 3–4 dozen small cookies, depending on your design of choice.

These cookies are rather small, so you may need to change your serving size.

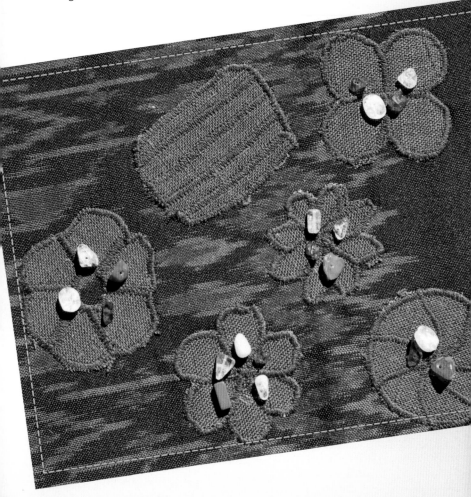

Iced Date Orange Drops

ONCE IN A WHILE I GET A CRAVING (I first typed crazing...is that a telling slip?) for a non-chocolate, fruity type cookie. This was a year of experimentation (at least cookie wise) so I did not immediately go for oatmeal. These are a little different, and great if you love dates. The dates are a natural sweetener, so these cookies have no refined sugar (without the icing), which is better for you! You can also vary the fruit, or skip the icing. It's all up to you.

INGREDIENTS

1/2 cup shortening, unsalted butter, or Earth Balance

1 tsp (or more) **ground cinnamon**

1 tsp orange zest, finely grated (if you don't have that, you can use ¼ teaspoon orange oil, or a little orange juice or another grated citrus zest. I think I had clementines at the time)

1/2 tsp baking soda

1 egg

1/2 cup honey

3 Tbsp orange juice

1 cup all purpose flour

1 cup whole wheat flour

1 cup chopped pitted dates (they are sticky to chop, so sorry)

ORANGE ICING:

1/2 cup confectioner's sugar

1 to 2 Tbsp orange juice

TO MAKE THE COOKIES

Preheat the oven to 350 degrees.

Cream the solidified fat in a mixer until smooth. Add the cinnamon, zest, and baking soda, and beat until combined. Beat in the egg, honey, and orange juice and then the flour. Stir in the dates.

Drop by spoonfuls onto lined cookie sheets, about 2 inches apart. These will spread. Bake until brown, 12–15 minutes. Let the cookies cool on racks.

To make the icing, stir together the sugar and orange juice until it is smooth. Ice cooled cookies.

Makes around 2 dozen.

Gingerbread Snowflakes

I LOVE GINGERBREAD. I am a big huge fan. Even though I am Jewish, I get caught up in the Winter Holiday Christmas cookie baking extravaganza. You are probably not surprised. Gingerbread is where I started making cut out cookies, and I would bake it year round if I weren't trying to vary a little. Most gingerbread recipes are too bland for my taste. At the risk of sounding like a *Cook's Illustrated* author (if you are not familiar, all their recipes start something like, "Could we make a cheese lasagna that didn't suck like everyone else's?" or, "Is it possible to make a yellow cake that is actually worth our time?"), I wanted to make a flavorful gingerbread that tasted as good as it looked before the Royal Icing. Then, you get the fun of decorating them, and with a little restraint, that is the best part. Here is my version.

INGREDIENTS

1/2 cup unsalted butter or Earth Balance, softened and cut into pieces

1/2 cup brown sugar

1/2 cup molasses

1 egg

1 tsp vanilla

2 cups all purpose flour

1 cups whole wheat flour

1 1/2 tsp baking powder

3/4 tsp baking soda

1/2 tsp salt

3 Tbsp ground cinnamon (depending on your love of cinnamon)

2 Tbsp ground ginger

1/2 tsp ground cloves

1/2 tsp nutmeg (fresh ground if you can)

TO MAKE THE COOKIES

In a food processor, pulse butter until creamy, and add brown sugar and molasses. Add egg and vanilla, and process further until smooth. You may have to scrape the bowl. In a large bowl, blend flours, baking soda, baking powder, salt, and spices until combined. Add in two parts to the butter mixture and blend until combined.

Then remove dough from processor and knead a little to get uniform dough. If the dough is still too sandy, melt 1 Tablespoon butter in the microwave. Make a little hole in your pile of dough, pour in the melted butter, and knead until you have a smooth dough. Divide in half, form balls and wrap in wax paper or plastic wrap (or your favorite reusable container). Flatten into discs and chill for at least 2 hours (all of preschool? Two swim lessons?) or overnight.

Preheat your oven to 375 degrees. Line cookie sheets or grease.

On a lightly floured work surface (you may need no flour), roll dough to 1/4 inch thickness and cut into snowflakes or other shapes as desired. My snowflake set allows me to make large and small snowflakes, with cut out interiors. If you have lots of time, you can even melt hard candies inside the holes to make a stained glass effect, if you have someone who will appreci-ate that. If you only want sprinkles, you can put them on now before you bake. Place the cookies 3/4 inch apart on cookie sheets. The cookies will not expand much, so don't be afraid to pack them in. Bake for 8–10 minutes or until just dry. If you like your gingerbread chewy, don't overbake. If you bake for too long, they will be crispy. If you take these out a minute or two early, you can always let them sit on the baking sheets for a few minutes longer to firm up.

Decorate with your favorite icing—either a quick mix of confectioner's sugar and water (I use about 1/4 cup confectioner's sugar to 1 teaspoon water, add more water to get a good consistency), or a fancier royal icing with egg whites (you can also buy a premade version of this). This is also a fine time to use col-ored sugar, sprinkles, or silver balls if you just ignore the sugar and coloring. Hey, it's only once a year, right?

Makes 1 dozen large or 2 dozen small cookies, depending on your cutters.

Madeleines

I GOT TO LIVE IN FRANCE FOR A SEMESTER DURING COLLEGE and so I have a soft spot for French baking (and who doesn't?) However, I was in Aix-en-Provence, and not Paris, so I got Calissons (a kind of traditional almond paste candy—*delicioux*!) and not Madeleines. Still, I always wanted to make these. I had never bought the pan before, though. Now I finally had an excuse. If you're really French, you would probably not substitute for unrefined flour, but I'm not so I did. You can even have them with a cup of tea instead of coffee if you prefer it. Hey, it's fusion cuisine.

INGREDIENTS

2 eggs

1/2 cup sugar

1 lemon, zest and juice—
    or 2 Tbsp lemon juice
    and 1/4 tsp lemon oil

2 tsp vanilla extract

1/4 cup whole wheat flour

1/2 cup all purpose flour

1/2 tsp baking powder

1 pinch salt

6 Tbsp butter (after all, they're French) **or Earth Balance** (*sacre bleu!*), melted and cooled

TO MAKE THE COOKIES

Spray your madeleine molds with cooking spray or grease and flour them slightly.

In a large bowl, combine the eggs with the sugar and beat on high (I use my hand mixer) about 6 minutes, or until thick and pale lemon yellow. Add the lemon juice and zest or oil and vanilla and beat until combined. Set aside.

In another small bowl, whisk the flours with the baking powder and salt. Sprinkle the dry ingredients on top of the egg mixture and slowly fold together with a silicone spatula. Add the melted butter and fold until just combined. Don't over mix—this is more like a pancake batter than chocolate chip cookies. Fill the molds.

Cover and chill for a few hours, until you can find a great deal on tickets to Paris online.

Preheat the oven to 400 degrees. Bake until the madeleines are golden on top, 11–13 minutes. Remove from oven, let cool a few minutes in molds, then unmold gently onto racks. *Bon Appetit!*

Makes 12 madeleines.

The BOM Cookies

THESE ARE MY HUSBAND DAVID'S FAVORITE COOKIES of the ones I could put in this book. His others involve espresso, which I didn't want to send to small children. The BOM stands for Chocolate Butterscotch Oatmeal Maple, but that was too long for a title. Anyway, I created these one weekend when we lived in Philadelphia before we had children, and between him and my friend's husband Russell, I think they ate the whole batch in a day. These are slightly different in that I threw in butterscotch chips (for variety)which makes them dairy (oops). If you leave that out, they are nondairy and very delicious as well.

INGREDIENTS

3/4 cup unsalted butter or Earth Balance, softened.

1/4 cup brown sugar

1/4 cup maple syrup

2 eggs

1 tsp vanilla

1/2 cup all purpose flour

1 cup whole wheat flour

1 tsp baking soda

1 tsp cinnamon

1/4 tsp salt

1/4 tsp ground nutmeg

3 cups oats

2 cups chocolate chips

1 cup butterscotch chips (optional, then just call them chocolate oatmeal maple)

TO MAKE THE COOKIES

Preheat the oven to 350 degrees. Line 2 cookie sheets. In a large bowl, beat the butter or Earth Balance with the sugar and maple syrup until creamy and smooth. Add each egg separately and then the vanilla, beat to blend. You may need to scrape down the sides of the bowl. Combine the flour, baking soda and spices in a separate bowl and then add to wet ingredients and mix well. Add oats and chips.

Drop by rounded spoonfuls onto lined cookie sheets, 2 inches apart.

Bake for 10 minutes or until lightly browned. Cool on wire racks. Watch them disappear.

Makes about 3 dozen. Make more, they won't last.

Almost Perfect Brownies

I AM FOREVER ON THE QUEST FOR THE PERFECT FUDGE BROWNIE.
In fact my sister bought me a brownie pan with just such a mission. I find
however, that as soon as I find the perfect brownie recipe, I lose the recipe.
This one works pretty well, but I'm not sure I'm done. These are pretty dense
and fudgy. Maybe I need to do a year of just brownies.

INGREDIENTS

3/4 cup unsalted butter or Earth Balance

4 oz. unsweetened chocolate, coarsely chopped

4 eggs

3/4 cup sugar

1 tsp vanilla extract

1 cup whole wheat flour

1/2 tsp baking powder

1/2 tsp salt

OPTIONAL: 1–2 cups chocolate chips

TO MAKE THE BROWNIES

Preheat the oven to 350 degrees. Spray a 9 x 13 inch baking pan with cooking
spray or butter it. Put the butter (or substitute) in a microwave proof bowl with
the chopped chocolate. Alternately, you can use a double boiler, but it requires
more cleaning. Melt the chocolate in 15 second increments in the microwave
until it can be stirred smooth. Let it cool.

In a large mixing bowl, beat the eggs and sugar together until thick and pale
yellow, at least 4 minutes (I use the hand mixer). It should leave a trail where
the beaters are lifted. Stir in the vanilla and melted chocolate until you get a
uniform color. Fold in the flour, baking powder, and salt. If more chocolate is
necessary, (and why not?) add the chocolate chips.

Pour the batter into the prepared pan and bake until a toothpick comes out
with some moist crumbs, 25–30 minutes. DO NOT OVERBAKE, or you will get
dry crumbly brownies instead of moist and chewy ones. You can start checking
after about 20 minutes. If you are not sure, they are probably done and you can
let them cool in the pan to finish.

Makes about 2 dozen bars, depending on the size of your cuts (and if you steal
the corners).

Chocolate Peanut Butter Bonbons or Buckeyes

MY SISTER IS ADDICTED TO PEANUT BUTTER. Really, she eats spoonfuls directly out of the jar, and so do her kids. She's even developing her own line of peanut butter. I think we're a foodie family. I'm not judging—in fact, I'm an enabler. So is she though, because she keeps buying me bakeware. These are not truly candy, but they look like it. They are easier to make than candy. I made these before the peanut allergy came up, and you could probably substitute almond butter.

INGREDIENTS

1/2 cup butter or Earth Balance, softened

1/2 cup crunchy peanut butter

1/2 cup brown sugar

1/4 tsp baking soda

1 egg

1 1/2 tsp vanilla extract

1 cup all purpose flour

1 1/2 cups whole wheat flour

12 oz. semisweet chocolate, chopped

2 tsp shortening or Earth Balance

TO MAKE THE COOKIES

In a large mixing bowl, beat the butter and peanut butter together with an electric mixer until well combined. I won't say smooth, because you will never get smooth, as the peanut butter is chunky. I wouldn't want to drive you crazy like that. Beat in the sugar and baking soda, then the egg and vanilla. Beat in all the flour until you have a thick dough.

Preheat the oven to 350 degrees. Line or grease 2 cookie sheets.

Shape the dough into 1 inch (or bigger) balls with slightly floured hands (or cocoa hands). You may need to wash your hands a few times if they get too sticky. Place the balls 2 inches apart on cookie sheets.

Bake until lightly browned on the bottom, 10 minutes.
Remove and let cool on a rack.

In a small, microwave safe bowl, heat the chocolate and shortening in 15 second bursts until melted together. Stir until smooth and cooled a little, but not so it hardens up again! Go check your email. Then, using tongs or a fork, dip each peanut butter ball in the chocolate until completely covered. Cool on a wax paper covered plate and then chill in the refrigerator until set. Send some to my sister. Makes 2–3 dozen.

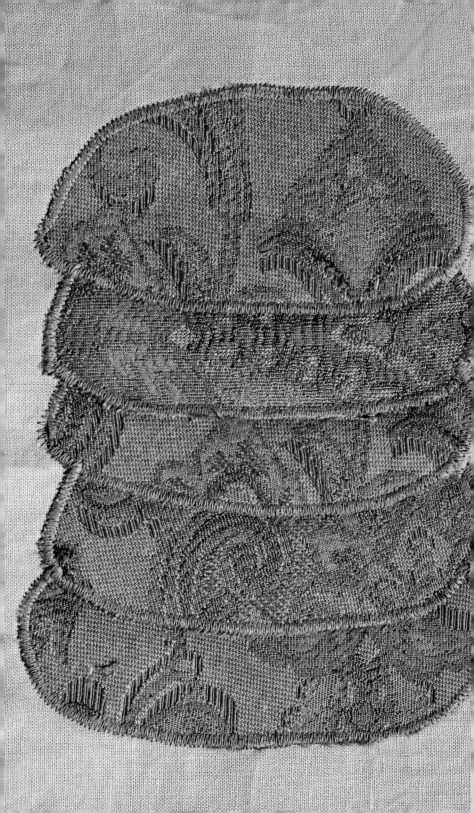

Pumpkin Cake Cookies

MY HUSBAND DAVID AND I used to live in Center City in Philadelphia near this amazing bakery called Petit 4. It was a dangerous place to live because they sold these banana chocolate chip cookies that were so amazing we would return to the neighborhood just for the cookies when we moved away from Philly and came back to visit. This is a diversion because these are not those cookies, but they have that same cakey consistency that makes them excellent for picnics and hard to stop eating. Once again, they have the delicious fall/winter spices that I can't stop using or eating. My kids love pumpkin soup as well as these cookies, so I guess I've passed on my love for that as well. I'll keep working on that other recipe though.

INGREDIENTS

1 Tbsp maple syrup

1 cup brown sugar

1/2 cup unsalted butter or Earth Balance, softened

1 egg

2 tsp vanilla extract

1 cup pumpkin puree — I used canned, but you could certainly buy, roast, and scoop your own pumpkin. I don't want to work that hard for cookies.

1 cup whole wheat flour

1 cup all purpose flour

1 tsp baking powder

1/4 tsp baking soda

1 tsp cinnamon

1/2 tsp cloves

1/2 tsp nutmeg

1 cup chocolate chips, optional

TO MAKE THE COOKIES

Preheat oven to 350 degrees. Line 2 cookie sheets with liners.

In a large mixing bowl, cream sugar, syrup, and butter (or substitute) until smooth. Add egg, vanilla, and pumpkin and beat until well blended. Mix in flour, baking powder, baking soda, and spices until you get a uniform dough. Stir in chocolate chips if using.

Drop spoonfuls of dough on cookie sheets 2 or 3 inches apart.
Bake 17 minutes, or until cookies have firmed up. Cool on wire racks.

Makes 2 dozen small cookies or fewer $3 bakery sized affairs.

Valentine Jam Sandwiches

THESE COOKIES WERE ANOTHER OUTLET for my cookie decorating obsession, and I got to buy new cookie cutters. These were hearts of different sizes so you could stack and cut out holes in larger cookies, creating a place for the jam to show through. They make beautiful gifts. You can use whatever jam you like and they will all be beautiful. If you can't have a week without chocolate, I suppose you could always use Nutella inside as well, and they won't be rejected.

These cookies use some whole wheat flour, although not as much as I usually put in. That means they won't be quite the golden yellowy color you may expect for a sugar cookie. They taste delicious however, and are that much better for you with whole grain in them. So, readjust your expectations and prepare to enjoy something new!

INGREDIENTS

1 cup butter or Earth Balance, softened

1 cup sugar or evaporated cane juice

1 egg

2 tsp vanilla extract

2 cups all purpose flour

1 cup whole wheat flour

1/2 tsp baking powder

1/2 tsp salt

1 to 2 Tbsp milk, coconut milk, soy milk, or almond milk

Egg for glazing—whisk slightly in a small bowl

All-fruit jam or preserves in your favorite flavor for filling. Now I happened to have a jar of locally made (OK, I made it) low-sugar raspberry freezer jam which I used. You may not have that. Most of the time, I don't either.

TO MAKE THE COOKIES

Preheat the oven to 350 degrees. Line your baking sheets with the liners of your choice.

In a large mixing bowl, cream the butter and sugar until well combined. Add the egg and vanilla and blend. In a smaller bowl, combine the flour, baking powder, and salt. Gradually add the dry ingredients to the butter mixture until well mixed. Drizzle in the liquid of your choice until the dough comes together and looks like a good dough. I know, terribly descriptive.

You don't have to chill this dough! You may want (or need—if the doorbell is ringing or something) to let them sit in the fridge for a few minutes, but they should be OK as is.

On a lightly floured board or flat surface of some kind (the stove top won't work), roll out the dough to 1/4 to 1/2 inch thickness. Cut into hearts, stars, love birds, cherubs—whatever strikes your Valentine fancy. I cut large base hearts, and more hearts for the top with cut outs in them so the jam would show through. Re-roll dough as needed.

Put the cookies on the sheets about 3/4 inch apart and glaze with the egg. They won't spread much. Bake for 20 minutes or until the bottoms are lightly browned. Thinner cookies will bake faster; thicker ones may take 30 minutes. Check after 20 minutes, I'd say.

Let cool on sheets, then spread jam over half the cookies, and top with the other half. Or whatever combination of tops and bottoms you have. Let set for a few minutes. Give to your sweetheart with milk or a White Russian, depending on the age of your sweetheart or the time of day.
If your sweetheart is lactose intolerant, try juice or champagne instead.

Makes 1 dozen beautiful, double-layer artwork cookies, or more smaller, delicate morsels.

Sesame Tea Cookies

THESE ARE ALONG THE SAME PRINCIPLE as peanut butter cookies, but have a slightly different flavor, and work perfectly for people who have a peanut allergy. They use tahini (sesame paste) that is available in my grocery store, and hopefully in yours. You could also make them with almond butter if you prefer. One taster remarked they would be delicious with tea, thus naming them.

INGREDIENTS

3/4 cup butter or Earth Balance

1/2 cup brown sugar

1 1/2 tsp baking powder

1/2 tsp nutmeg

1 egg

3 Tbsp tahini

1 Tbsp honey

1 tsp vanilla extract

1 cup whole wheat flour

1 2/3 cups all purpose flour

1/3 cup sesame seeds

TO MAKE THE COOKIES

Preheat the oven to 375 degrees. Line or grease 2 cookie sheets.

In a large mixing bowl, cream the butter until smooth and, well, creamy. Add the sugar, baking powder, and nutmeg, and mix until combined. Beat in the egg, then add the tahini, honey, and vanilla, and blend well. Add the flour and beat until you get a uniform dough. Stir in the sesame seeds.

Shape the dough into 1–2 inch balls and place 2 inches apart on cookie sheets. Press the balls down with a fork first one way, then perpendicular to the first press, so you get a crisscross.

Bake 10–12 minutes, or until lightly browned. Cool on racks.

Makes around 2 dozen peanut-free cookies.

Chocolate Peppermint Chunk Cookies

YOU WILL NOTICE THROUGHOUT THIS BOOK that there is a lot of the chocolate/peppermint combination. It is a favorite of mine, and my friend Sherry admitted the same. So I kept throwing it in. If peppermint is not a particularly pleasant taste to you, feel free to substitute nuts, or cut up candy bars, or chunks of meat if that would be better.

INGREDIENTS

1 cup all purpose flour

1 1/4 cups whole wheat flour (you will really not notice the whole wheat with the chocolate flavor, especially if you use a pastry flour)

3/4 cup unsweetened cocoa (I prefer Dagoba)

1 tsp baking soda

1/2 tsp salt

1 cup butter or Earth Balance, softened

1/4 cup brown sugar

1/2 cup sugar

2 eggs

1 tsp vanilla

1 cup chocolate chips

1 cup smashed candy canes (do it in a bag, on the garage floor, with a hammer, and not so much that you make holes in the bag and lose the candy. And not with the rope in the study.* Try to get chunks that are about the same size as your chocolate chips)

*Random reference to Clue

TO MAKE THE COOKIES

Preheat the oven to 375 degrees. Line two cookie sheets with reusable liners or parchment paper.

In a large bowl, combine the flours, cocoa, baking soda, and salt. In a large mixing bowl, with the electric mixer, cream the butter or butter-like fat with the sugars. Blend until smooth, then add the eggs and vanilla and mix until all combined. Add the dry ingredients all at once and then slowly blend to make a uniform dough. Mix in the chocolate chips and the peppermint chunks.

Place teaspoonsful of dough 2 inches apart on the cookie sheets. Bake for 10 minutes or until the bottoms are dry and the whole kitchen smells like chocolate.

Cool on a rack. Makes around 3 dozen.

Mojito Cookies

THESE ARE A LITTLE UNUSUAL, but when you're making a year's worth of cookie recipes, sometimes you have to branch out a bit. Lime is an alternative to the more frequently used lemon, but it's very refreshing and delicious. These would be great in the middle of the summer, but of course I made them in February. I was probably dreaming of summer. The recipe is also greatly changed from what I actually mailed, but they morphed in the testing. It was that kind of week I guess. They are also quick, dump-into-the-bowl kind of cookies if you skip chilling, so they're perfect for a cookie emergency. Thanks to Amy Michael, who reminded me about the mint—I was too focused on the rum part of the cocktail.

INGREDIENTS

1 cup butter or Earth Balance, softened

1/2 cup sugar

1/2 tsp baking soda

1/2 tsp grated lime zest or lime oil

1/4 cup lime juice

2 Tbsp dark rum

1 egg

2 Tbsp finely chopped fresh mint

1 1/4 cups all purpose flour

1 1/2 cups whole wheat flour

LIME GLAZE:

1/2 cup confectioners sugar

2 Tbsp melted butter or Earth Balance

1 Tbsp lime juice (or lime oil or lemon juice or other flavoring)

2 tsp dark rum

2 drops mint extract

TO MAKE THE COOKIES

Preheat the oven to 375 degrees. Line cookie sheets with liners.

In a large mixing bowl, cream the butter or substitute until smooth. Add the sugar, baking soda, and lime zest and continue to beat. Add the lime juice, rum, egg, chopped mint, and finally the flour. Mix until all combined. Divide dough in half, shape into logs (about 3 inches in diameter), wrap and chill for an hour, or until after your pedicure.

Slice the cookie dough into 1/4 inch slices and place on the cookie sheets, 2 inch apart. Bake 10–12 minutes or until edges are browned and bottoms are dry.

Remove and cool on wire racks.

Whisk together the glaze ingredients, adding more juice if needed to make a smooth glaze. Drizzle on cooled cookies.

Use remaining mint to whip up mojitos for full effect.

Makes about 3 dozen.

Renamed Bars

MY MOTHER ALWAYS QUOTED one of her favorite cookbooks, saying, "If it doesn't work out the way you planned, just rename it." Okay, this is a week that never got posted on Facebook, because this was the week that we went to my husband's conference in Snowmass, CO (yes, a pretty nice place for a conference). We rented a house and I was in someone else's kitchen. I still wanted to make cookies though, I was determined not to miss a week. So I thought, "Hey, something no-bake, then I won't need lots of ingredients and mess and someone else's kitchen tools." Ha! You can follow this recipe if you want, but mostly you can just learn from my failure, and try a different one.

INGREDIENTS

1 box chocolate wafer cookies
like chocolate Graham crackers or chocolate Annie's bunny crackers. (Why I didn't just send those, I don't know.) Crushed into a fine meal.

1 cup walnuts, pecans, hazelnuts, or almonds, finely chopped. Don't tell, but I used their coffee grinder to do this.

1 cup confectioner's sugar, because chocolate cookies aren't sweet enough.

1/3 cup flavoring or liquor.
Depends who they are for. Try Bailey's, or coffee, or if you want it just for kids, almond milk. As long as they don't have a nut allergy.

1 to 2 Tbsp water

5 oz. bittersweet or semisweet chocolate, chopped. Whatever you can find in the local grocery store. If it has to be Baker's chocolate or even Nestle's, so be it.

1 Tbsp Earth Balance, butter, or shortening.

6 oz. white chocolate,
if you have to, chopped

TO MAKE THE BARS

In a large mixing bowl (OK, found that), stir together the chocolate cookie crumbs (they were smashed with a hammer and not that uniform), chopped nuts, confectioner's sugar, and liquid flavoring. Add a little water to form into balls. Okay, this was not working. The crumbs were too big and I sort of shaped small balls but they didn't seem stable. Hmm. OK, close enough. Place on a cookie sheet (no, a plate) lined with wax paper. Got it.

Next, in a small saucepan, heat the semisweet chocolate and butter over LOW heat until melted. In another small saucepan, do the same with the white chocolate. OK, a larger saucepan. Go with what you have. Don't try to do this simultaneously. Wait, oops, white chocolate is forming into a sticky crusty mess, turn down the heat, oops, dark chocolate smoking and getting chunky. Shoot. OK, add more Earth Balance to the white chocolate, heat it up again, no, let it cool, no, no, um...heat slowly, stirring all the time, and add more Earth Balance. OK, um, that sort of works.

With a fork, dip the balls into the dark chocolate and ...watch them crumble when you stick the fork into them. Well.

OK, try again. Find a brownie pan. Line with foil or wax paper. Spread the misshapen balls of nuts and cookie crumbs into the bottom of it. Chill in the fridge for an hour, or until you stop pulling your hair in frustration and wondering why you decided to bake on vacation. Reheat (slowly) the dark chocolate in the microwave (in a microwave safe bowl, silly) for 15 seconds and stir. If it doesn't stir, heat another 5 seconds and stir until it does. Drizzle the chocolate over the nut mixture. Repeat with white chocolate (a new bar if you added too much butter).

Chill in the fridge while you take a nap. Cut into bars and enjoy.

Makes: some. Don't ask me, the bars weren't even.

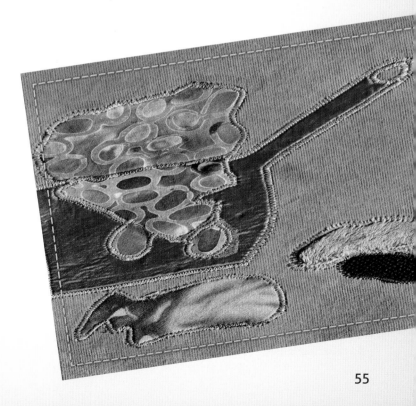

Hamantaschen

THERE ARE MANY VARIETIES OF HAMANTASCHEN, a traditional folded, fruit-jam-filled cookie made for the Jewish holiday of Purim, which typically falls in March of the American calendar. The translation is "Haman's Pockets," although they are shaped to be like a tri-cornered hat. Don't ask. In any event, Haman is the evil character in the story, the Jews defeat him, we eat cookies. And dress up and drink. Really, it's like Jewish Mardi Gras. Except, instead of throwing beads, Jews are required to give gifts of food to their friends and to the poor in honor of the holiday.

Thus, back to cookies (that last well in packages). Whether you fill them with prune or poppy seed jam (the traditional) or peanut butter chips (my sister), they are fun to make, give, and eat. I usually make a triple recipe. This recipe has been passed to me multiple times by my mother. Now I have it in a book and (maybe) won't lose it again.

INGREDIENTS

1 cup whole wheat flour

1 to 1 1/4 cups all purpose flour

2 tsp baking powder

1/2 cup shortening or Earth Balance (they are traditionally made non dairy, following the Jewish rules of Kashrut, because they are meant to be eaten after a meat meal. If this does not effect you, by all means, use butter)

1 cup honey or 1/2 cup honey and 1/2 cup sugar

1/4 tsp salt

1 Tbsp orange juice

1 tsp vanilla

1 Tbsp orange rind

2 eggs

FILLING:

Solo poppy seed, prune or apricot pie filling (in a can)

OR

Apricot jam, peanut butter, chocolate chips, raspberry jam, or some other filling, just make sure it's not too liquidy so it won't run out of the cookies.

TO MAKE THE COOKIES

In a large mixing bowl, cream the shortening and sugar or honey until creamy and smooth. Add eggs and beat. Add orange juice, rind, and vanilla and beat thoroughly. Mix flour, baking powder, and salt together in a medium bowl and then add slowly to the honey mixture. Mix until you get a uniform, thick dough. Add extra flour if needed to make a smooth, workable dough. Divide into balls, flatten, and wrap in wax paper or store in Tupperware in the fridge. Chill until you feel chill (at least an hour)

Preheat oven to 400 degrees. Line 2 or 3 cookie sheets.

Flour a board and a rolling pin. Roll out dough to 1/8 inch thickness. Cut out 2 inch circles using a cookie cutter or a washed (and dried) overturned glass. If it had beer in it, try again. In the center of each circle, place a baby food spoon size dollop of filling—maybe 1/2 a teaspoon. I guess it depends on your baby. Anyway, you don't want the filling to squeeze out the edges. Take one third of the circle and turn it up over the filling. Take the other two sides of the circle and squeeze edges to form a triangle. Make sure the corners are well-sealed or they will come apart while baking. Follow the picture. Place 1 inch apart on the cookie sheets and bake 12 minutes or until edges are beginning to brown and bottoms are dry. If some filling leaks out, eat those yourself, but wait a few minutes, jam out of the oven will burn your mouth.

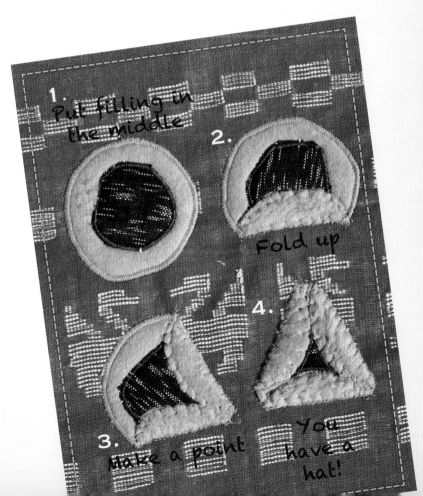

1. Put filling in the middle

2. Fold up

3. Make a point

4. You have a hat!

Peanut Brittle Crunch Cookies

I FEAR THIS MAY HAVE BEEN the week that spurred Sherry's son's peanut allergy. Different son. I didn't know, and I don't think she did either. If you are allergic to peanuts, don't make these! If not, they are delicious and crunchy... hopefully with no unpleasant surprises.

INGREDIENTS

1 cup butter or Earth Balance, softened

3/4 cup brown sugar

1/4 cup maple syrup

1/2 tsp baking soda

2 eggs

1 cup chunky peanut butter

1 tsp vanilla extract

1 cup all purpose flour

1 1/4 cups whole wheat flour

7 or 8 oz. package peanut brittle (I got mine from our local candy store, if you don't have peanut brittle, you could substitute a toffee candy like Skor bars or something like that)

OPTIONAL: 1 cup crushed peanut butter covered pretzels for extra crunch and peanut butter flavor, in case you don't have enough. In my market, these are available in bulk next to yogurt and chocolate-covered pretzels.

TO MAKE THE COOKIES

Preheat the oven to 375 degrees and line 2 cookie sheets.

In a large mixing bowl, cream the butter or Earth Balance (This book is not sponsored by Earth Balance, but I do use it a lot!) and beat until smooth. Add the sugar, maple syrup, and baking soda, and beat until combined. Add the eggs, peanut butter, and vanilla and beat thoroughly. Beat in the flour until mixed, and then stir in the peanut brittle and pretzels if using.

Drop the dough on the cookie sheets by rounded teaspoonfuls, 2 inches apart. Bake until golden on top, about 10 minutes. Cool on racks.

Makes about 3 dozen crunchy treats.

Chocolate Praline Cookies

ANOTHER COOKIE for those who love pecans, and an easy week after the fussy Hamantaschen. They are crunchy little pecan treats.

INGREDIENTS

1/2 cup butter or Earth Balance, softened

1/2 cup brown sugar

2 teaspoons baking powder

1 egg

2 teaspoons vanilla extract

1 cup all purpose flour

1/2 cup whole wheat flour

1 cup toasted (first I typed tasted, that too) **chopped pecans**

TOPPING:

1/2 cup semisweet chocolate chips (Sunrise if you need non-dairy)

1 teaspoon Earth Balance or butter

TO MAKE THE COOKIES

Preheat the oven to 375 degrees. Line 2 cookie sheets with silicone liners or parchment.

In a large mixing bowl, cream the butter or substitute until creamy. Beat in the sugar and baking powder, then the egg and vanilla. Beat in flour until you have a uniform dough. Finally, mix in the nuts.

Drop the dough by teaspoonfuls 2 inches apart on the cookie sheets. Bake until bottoms are dry and golden brown, about 12–15 minutes. Remove from sheets and cool on a rack.

To make the topping, melt the chocolate with the butter in a microwavable bowl for 25 seconds, repeating in 10–second increments and stirring in between until the chocolate is smooth. With a baby spoon, drizzle the chocolate over the cooled cookies. Alternately, put the chocolate in a tiny pitcher and pour over the cookies; it might be less messy.

Makes a small 2 dozen, or larger 1 and a half dozen.

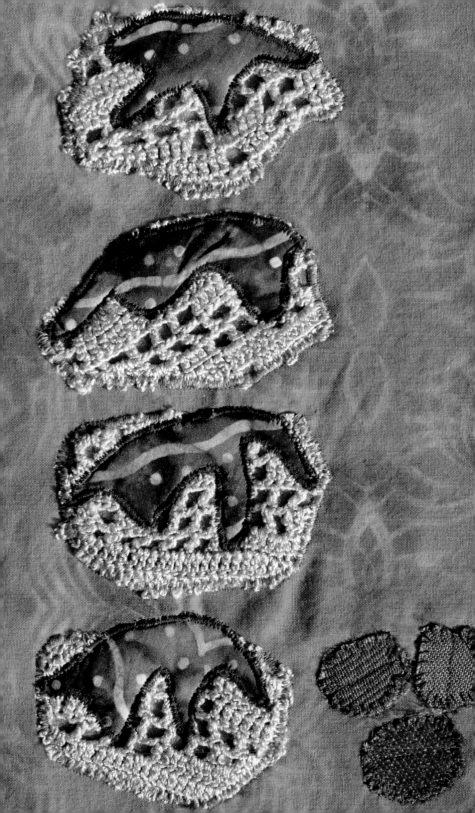

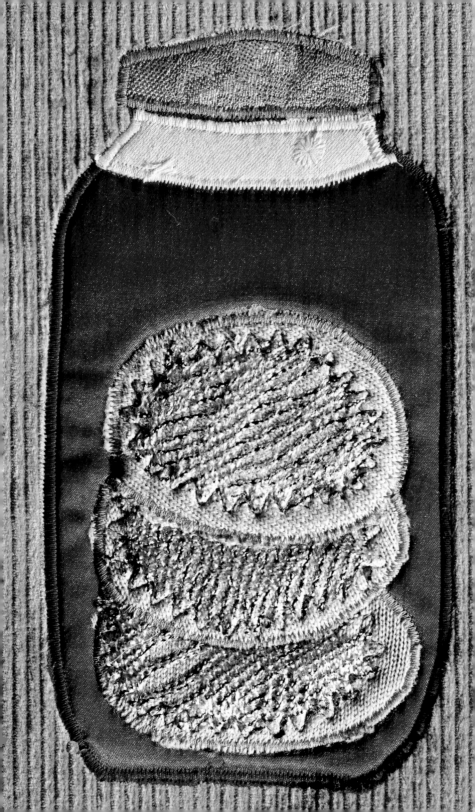

Vanilla Spice Cookies

THESE ARE GUSSIED- UP SUGAR COOKIES, just for a little variation. The original inspiration had rum in it, but as I was baking for children, I eliminated it. As the year went on though, I decided a little rum wasn't so bad for the kids. You can always add it back in, instead of the vanilla. Or you could go crazy with ginger or cinnamon liquor.

INGREDIENTS

3/4 cup butter or Earth Balance, softened

3/4 cup sugar

1 tsp baking powder

1/2 tsp baking soda

1/2 tsp allspice

1/2 tsp cinnamon

1/2 tsp nutmeg

1 egg

1/4 cup honey

2 tsp vanilla or maple extract or 3 Tablespoons maple syrup. With the larger amount of liquid you may need a touch more flour.

1 cup all purpose flour

1 2/3 cups whole wheat flour

TOPPING:

1/8 cup sugar or turbinado sugar

3/4 tsp allspice

TO MAKE THE COOKIES

In a large mixing bowl, cream the butter until smooth. Add in sugar, baking powder, baking soda, and spices. Beat in the egg, honey, and flavoring of your choice. Beat in flour until it is all incorporated. Divide in half, roll into logs. My logs were about 8 inches long, which yielded final cookies about 3 inches across (after baking). Make wider or thinner depending on how big you want your finished cookies.

On a small plate, combine the topping sugar and allspice. Roll each log in the mixture, wrap in wax paper, and chill in the refrigerator long enough to watch 2 episodes of *Glee*. Save the remaining sugar mixture.

Preheat the oven to 375 degrees and line 2 cookie sheets.

Cut the logs into 1/4 inch thick slices and place the slices 2 inches apart on the cookie sheets. Sprinkle with the remaining sugar and bake 10 minutes, or until lightly browned.

Cool cookies on a rack.

Makes about 40 cookies.

Chocolate Peppermint Stripes

THESE ARE MORE SHAPE, SLICE, AND BAKE flavored shortbread cookies. You may have noticed that Sherry said she loved chocolate and peppermint, so I couldn't help but comply. These have an unholy amount of butter, but that's what makes shortbread work, in my experience.

INGREDIENTS

1 1/4 cups butter or Earth Balance, softened

2/3 cup sugar

1/2 tsp baking powder

1 cup all purpose flour

1 cup whole wheat flour

2 oz. Bittersweet chocolate, melted and cooled

1/2 tsp peppermint extract

TO MAKE THE COOKIES

In a large mixing bowl, cream the butter until smooth. Beat in the sugar and baking powder. Beat in the flour until all combined. Divide the dough in half, and place in bowls. In one bowl, add the chocolate and knead the dough with your hands until the chocolate is all combined. In the other bowl, add the peppermint and knead to combine. Shape each dough into a disc, wrap in waxed paper and chill two hours or until the baby wakes up from (a very long) nap. If you chill too long, they won't be easy to handle, and you will have to let them warm up a bit before shaping.

On a lightly floured board or other flat surface (not your brother), divide each half of the dough in half. Now you have four pieces. Pat each piece flat into a 10 by 3 inch rectangle, approximately. Stack on top of each other, alternating flavors, so you have a chocolate and peppermint stack. Chill another hour. Check the mail, recycle most of it.

Preheat the oven to 375 degrees and line 2 cookie sheets with silicone liners or parchment paper.

Remove cookies from fridge, turn stack sidewise and slice into 1/4 inch thick slices. Slices should look like the picture. Place 2 inches apart on the cookie sheets. If they come apart, press back together firmly.

Bake until the bottoms are browned and dry, 10 minutes. Cool on a rack. Makes about 20.

65

Matzah Praline Bars

OKAY, SO THIS WEEK IS A LITTLE UNUSUAL. This is how I can really see the rhythms of a year in cookies. This cookie was during the Jewish holiday of Passover, or Pesach, which commemorates the exodus from Egypt. For a week, observant Jews don't eat any bread or bread products, wheat (except matzah, a flat bread baked quickly and without yeast so it won't rise), rice, corn, there's a whole list. It's supposed to remind us of how the Jews had to leave Egypt so fast they didn't even have time for bread to rise. In my tradition, I don't keep any of these products in my house at all during the holiday. So, how, you ask, do cookies come into this picture? Well, Jews are supposed to commemorate the festival, but not in a mourning sort of way, in a celebratory way. So although we can't have wheat, dessert definitely has to be in the picture. This usually involves an unholy amount of egg whites whipped for a ridiculously long amount of time and added to a heart healthy amount of potato starch or dark chocolate. Potatoes are allowed. However, the most common kind of Passover cookies are meringues or macaroons—lots of egg whites- which don't do so well with mailing. So, I found a version of this recipe (thanks to Susie Fishbein) and tried it out. I'm not sure it was the greatest mailer either, but I digress. It definitely has potential, and I might even venture to say that I would eat them when it isn't Passover as well. Still, I was happy to get to week 32 and pull out my flour again.

INGREDIENTS

3 to 4 whole squares of matzah (right out of the package, whole wheat, white, or egg, your choice)

1 cup butter or Earth Balance (the soy free is still OK for Passover, depending on how strict you are, there are also other brands of just-for-Passover dairy-free margarine)

3/4 cup brown sugar

12 oz. bittersweet chocolate or dairy-free chocolate chips, chopped (Not unsweetened) (I like the way bar chocolate melts better)—Get the best you can find for Passover; this recipe is all in the chocolate

1 cup finely chopped nuts (pecans or almonds are excellent)

Butter/margarine/oil for greasing

TO MAKE THE BARS

Preheat the oven to 325 degrees. Cover a cookie sheet with aluminum foil or a silicone liner and then oil/butter/grease it a lot. The caramel will stick, believe me.

Place the matzahs down on the sheet, covering it as much as possible. You can break up pieces if you need to.

In a medium saucepan, melt the butter and then add the sugar: here's the key part: STIR constantly, not absentmindedly like I did, burning the caramel. Stir, stir, stir, until the sugar boils and thickens to a nice caramel consistency, but doesn't boil over and ruin your stovetop. It will happen quickly, so watch. Turn off the heat, stir some more, and then carefully pour over the matzahs.

Bake for 12 minutes, then remove from the oven and sprinkle the chopped chocolate over the caramel part. Reduce the heat to 250 degrees, and bake for another 10 minutes. Spread the chocolate to make a nice even layer. Finally, sprinkle the nuts over the chocolate and place the whole thing in the refrigerator or freezer (you may have to remove the foil from your tray if you have a side by side fridge/freezer like I do—use a mitt and don't burn your hands!).

Chill for a while (while you catch up on email or bake a kugel) and then break into pieces. Store in the fridge or an airtight container.

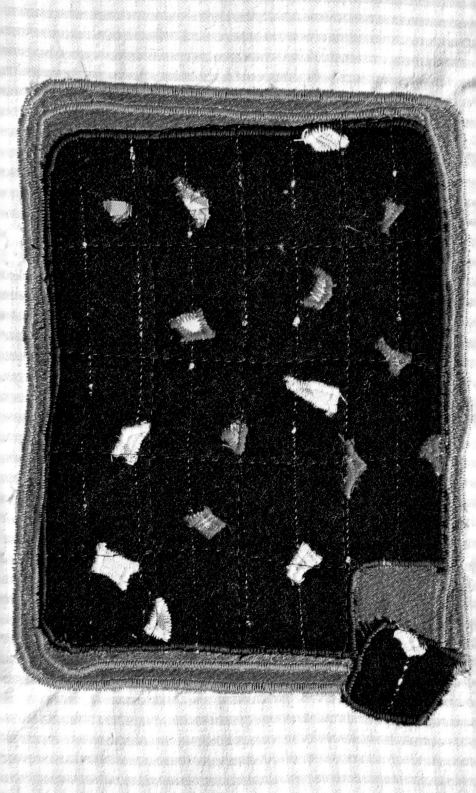

Chocolate Peppermint Brownies

I AM FOREVER ON THE QUEST for the perfect brownie, but I also think (apologies to my sister) that chocolate and peppermint is the world's best combination. I found out during this year that Sherry was of the same mind, and have you ever found non-dairy peppermint brownies in an ordinary bakery? Good luck. So, I tried these out. Also, I don't like brownies with nuts, but if you do, feel free to add.

INGREDIENTS

1/2 cup butter or dairy free margarine

6 1/2 oz. unsweetened chocolate, chopped

3 eggs

3/4 cup sugar

1 tsp vanilla extract

1 cup all purpose flour

1/2 cup whole wheat flour

1/3 cup unsweetened cocoa powder

2 to 3 large peppermint candy canes, crushed. (Go ahead, put them in a plastic bag and give your preschooler a mallet.)

TO MAKE THE BROWNIES

Preheat the oven to 350 degrees and line a 9 by 13 pan with parchment or foil. Spray the parchment with cooking spray.

In a saucepan or microwave, melt the chopped chocolate with the butter or substitute (in 20–30 second increments in the microwave or slowly stirring over low heat). Let it cool.

In a large mixing bowl, beat the eggs with the sugar and vanilla until smooth, thick, and creamy. Pour the cooled chocolate into the egg mixture and mix together with a wooden spoon until combined. Resist eating now. Add both flours and mix well. Add the cocoa and peppermint stick and stir.

Pour into the pan and spread until the top is smooth.

Bake until edges are slightly dry, 25–30 minutes. I prefer undercooked brownies to overcooked, a little extra fudginess is never bad. Cool on a wire rack, cut into bars. Careful, the peppermint might be a bit stringy.

Makes 2 dozen small or one giant bar.

Kitchen Sink Cookies

THIS WAS PRETTY MUCH A THROW IT ALL IN kind of recipe. Some people call these hermit cookies, maybe if you were holed up in the woods by yourself for months at a time, you could survive on these and a little water. You can pretty much throw in whatever you have in your pantry. Except maybe uncooked noodles and curry paste. But hey, try it sometime if you like.

INGREDIENTS

1/2 cup butter or Earth Balance, softened

1/2 cup brown sugar

1 Tbsp honey

2 eggs

1 tsp vanilla extract

1/2 tsp orange juice

1/2 tsp lemon extract or juice

1 cup whole wheat flour

3/4 cups white flour

1/2 cup rolled oats

3/4 tsp baking powder

1/4 tsp baking soda

1/4 tsp salt

OPTIONS (use one or more):

2 tsp cinnamon

3/4 tsp nutmeg

1 1/2 cups raisins

3/4 to 1 cup chopped dates

1 cup chocolate chips (why not?)

1 cup cinnamon chips (if you can find them)

1/2 crushed cinnamon candy

1 cup cranberries

TO MAKE THE COOKIES

Preheat the oven to 350 degrees. Line two cookie sheets with silicone liners or parchment paper.

In a large mixing bowl, cream the butter or butter-like substance with the sugar until smooth and creamy. Add the honey, eggs, vanilla, and citrus. Then, fold in all the rest of the ingredients except the fruit and candy. Blend until you get a uniform dough and then mix in the chips, raisins and dates and potato chips. OK, maybe not everything in the pantry. Put spoonfuls of dough 2 inches apart on the cookie sheets.

Bake 18–20 minutes or until browned on the bottom. Remove and let the cookies cool on a rack.

Makes 2 dozenish.

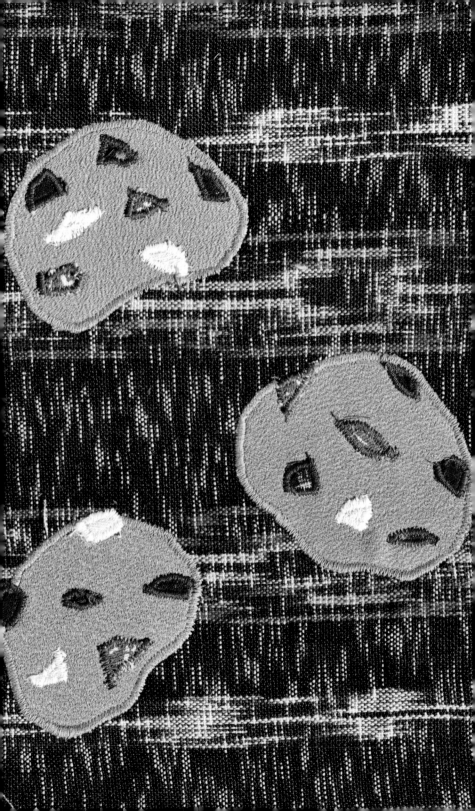

Berry Shortbread

I GENERALLY DON'T LIKE making traditional shortbread, at least most of the recipes I've tried. I find it too fussy, often too crumbly, and hard to work with, just like traditional pie crust. Actually, they're pretty similar. (On a side note, try *Cook's Illustrated's* no-fail pie crust for one that is really excellent.) Anyway, I gave shortbread a shot, but I ended up adding an egg to the original recipe for these to make the dough more workable. So no, it's not really shortbread. But it's yummy!

INGREDIENTS

- 1/2 cup whole wheat flour
- 3/4 cup all purpose flour
- 3 Tbsp sugar
- 1 tsp orange zest or 1/8 teaspoon orange oil

- 3/4 cup butter or Earth Balance
- 1/4 cup raspberry, boysenberry, strawberry, blackberry, or mixed berry jam. Really, any berry.
- 1 egg, slightly beaten

TO MAKE THE COOKIES

Preheat the oven to 325 degrees. Line a cookie sheet.

Do this by hand: In a large mixing bowl, stir together the flour, sugar, and orange product. With a pastry blender (a very nifty little gadget that's like four dull blades attached to a handle) or a fork, cut in the butter until your dough resembles fine crumbs. That's what the recipes always say. It should look mealy.

Divide in half and knead—it may be a crumbly mess. Add the egg and knead into a smooth dough.

Shape each half into an 8 inch log and place on the cookie sheets. Pat the logs until they are about 2 inches wide and then make a groove in the middle of each with the back of a teaspoon.

Bake until the edges start to brown, 25 minutes. Immediately (well, remove from oven first) spoon the jam into the indentation. Cut the strips diagonally into bars.

Makes about 16. They go quickly.

Carrot Cranberry Drops

THESE ARE LIKE LITTLE CARROT CAKES in a cookie. You could add cream cheese frosting, but I didn't think it would travel well.

INGREDIENTS

1 cup butter or Earth Balance

1/2 cup brown sugar

1/4 cup maple syrup

1 tsp baking soda

2 tsp cinnamon

1 tsp orange zest or
   1/4 tsp orange oil

1/2 tsp ground ginger

1/2 tsp nutmeg

2 eggs

1 tsp vanilla

1 1/4 cups whole wheat flour

1/2 cup all purpose flour

1 1/2 cups shredded carrots

1 cup oats

1 cup dried cranberries or other
   dried fruit

1/2 cup chopped walnuts or pecans
   (optional for those of you who like
   nuts)

TO MAKE THE COOKIES

Preheat the oven to 375 degrees. Line two cookie sheets with silicone liners or parchment paper.

In a large mixing bowl, cream the butter or butter substitute until smooth. Add brown sugar, maple syrup, baking soda, cinnamon, orange zest or oil, ginger, and nutmeg and beat until smooth. Then, beat in eggs, vanilla, and the flour. Stir in carrots, oats, cranberries, and possibly the nuts until you have a good dough.

Drop the dough onto the cookie sheets by teaspoons, 2 inches apart.
Bake 10 minutes, or until browned on top. Cool on racks.

Makes 2–3 dozen. Watch out for Bugs Bunny.

Lemon Letters

APPARENTLY THIS IS A SERIES OF COOKIES that taste like or are made to resemble other things. These are like lemon meringue pie you can pack in your lunch.

INGREDIENTS

1 cup unsalted butter or Earth Balance, softened

1/2 cup sugar

2 egg yolks

Juice and zest from 2 lemons, divided

3/4 tsp lemon oil or lemon extract

1/4 tsp salt

1/4 tsp baking powder

1 cup whole wheat flour

1 1/4 cups all purpose flour

TOPPING:

The two egg whites

1/3 cup sugar

The leftover zest

TO MAKE THE COOKIES

Cream the butter with the sugar in a large mixing bowl until smooth and creamy. Beat in the egg yolks, then add the lemon zest from one lemon and the juice from both, the lemon oil, salt, and baking powder. Beat in the flour. Divide in half, roll into 2 balls, and flatten into discs. Wrap or otherwise cover and chill in the fridge 3 hours or until you finish whichever Harry Potter you are reading (this is going to very much date this book—the last movie just came out).

Meanwhile, make the meringue topping:

Whip egg whites until soft peaks form, then add sugar and continue to whip until you have stiff peaks where the tips of the whites stand up. This is an excellent task for your more experienced 4 1/2–year-old sous chef, one who doesn't lick the bowl.

Preheat the oven to 350 degrees and prepare cookie sheets by lining them with silicone liners or parchment paper.

On a lightly floured board or other smooth, flat surface, roll out the dough to less than a 1/4 inch thick and cut into shapes.

Place 1 inch apart on sheets.

Spoon a baby spoons' worth meringue topping on each cookie and spread to cover the cookie. Add more as necessary. Sprinkle with the remaining zest.

Bake the cookies until the meringue is lightly browned, 12–15 minutes. Cool on a rack.

Makes 2–3 dozen depending on the size of your cutters.

Chocolate Spice Drops

EVERY FEW WEEKS I have to make sure that I have made enough chocolate. In all spice cookies, increase the spices if you like it that way. I am a big cinnamon fan, so I usually start with twice the recommended amount. I've listed that for you. It gives the cookies more of a Mexican chocolate flair. Also, the original recipe called for whiskey, but you can substitute any spirit you like. This was also the week of my new oven, so that was the inspiration for my illustration, as you can see. Note: These cookies can be made vegan if that is appealing to you. They have spice and chocolate, so no one will notice.

INGREDIENTS

1 cup all purpose flour

1 cup whole wheat flour

1/2 cup brown sugar

1/2 cup unsweetened cocoa powder
(I use Dagoba)

1 tsp ground cinnamon

1/2 tsp ground cloves

1/2 tsp baking powder

1/4 tsp baking soda

1/4 tsp salt

3/4 cup milk, soy milk, almond milk, or coconut milk

1/2 cup canola oil

1 Tbsp Ginger liquor.

1 cup semisweet chocolate chips
(I used Sunspire organic which have no milk)

TO MAKE THE COOKIES

Put the flour, sugar, cocoa, cinnamon, cloves, baking powder, baking soda, and salt in a large mixing bowl, and stir to combine. Add the liquid ingredients and beat until well blended. Mix in the chocolate chips.

Chill in freezer for 15 minutes, or in fridge for an hour or longer if you have to pick up your kid and drive him to swimming lessons or piano. They'll forgive you (the cookies).

Preheat the oven to 400 degrees. Line or grease 2 baking sheets. Scoop approximately one teaspoon of dough and form into a ball. Place a couple of inches apart on baking sheet. These won't spread much. Bake for 10 minutes or until the cookies look puffy and dry. If they are still gooey, add a couple of minutes. Remove from the oven and cool on racks.

Makes 2–3 dozen, depending on exact size.

Maple Pecan Crunch Cookies

THESE HAVE TO BE DEDICATED to my husband David, because although they are not his favorite cookie (since I had never made them before this year) they feature his two favorite things: Pecans, and Maple Syrup. He recommends using butter if you can. They are sort of like pecan pie without the trouble, and a lot less fat. There are all sorts of recommendations for making slice and bake cookies perfectly round, such as chilling them in half of a paper towel roll. I don't care enough about the shape to fuss with that. You can slice and shape as you like and they are delightful. If you want to fuss, go ahead.

INGREDIENTS

1 cup all purpose flour

1 1/2 cups whole wheat flour

1/2 tsp salt

1/4 tsp baking soda

3/4 cup unsalted butter or Earth Balance, softened

1/4 cup sugar

1/4 cup brown sugar

1/4 cup maple syrup (the more flavorful, the better—if you have local maple syrup, fantastic)

1 egg

1 tsp vanilla extract

2 cups toasted pecans, coarsely chopped (I forgot to toast mine, they came out fine)

GLAZE:

A slight 1/4 cup confectioner's sugar

1/4 cup warm maple syrup

TO MAKE THE COOKIES

In a medium mixing bowl, combine the flours, salt, and baking soda. Set aside. In a stand mixer, beat the butter or Earth Balance until creamy and smooth. Add the sugars and maple syrup. Mix until blended, then add the egg and the vanilla. Scrape the bowl as needed. Slowly mix in the dry ingredients until combined and then add the pecans.

Divide the dough into three parts and roll into log shapes, so the ends are about the size you would like for finished cookies. You may need to flour your surface a little. My logs were about 2 inches around. Cover with your favorite wrap and chill until firm, 3 hours or overnight, or at least until after school.

Preheat the oven to 350 degrees. Line cookie sheets with silicone liners or parchment, or grease them. Slice the logs into discs about 1/4 inch wide (after taking off the plastic wrap!) using a small serrated knife. Place the cookies on baking sheets 1 inch apart and bake until lightly browned, 20 minutes.

While the cookies are baking, make the glaze. Stir the confectioner's sugar into the maple syrup and whisk until combined. You can add a little water or more maple syrup until you get the right consistency.

Remove the cookies from the oven and set to cool. Brush on the glaze with a pastry brush while the cookies are still warm. Then remove to a rack and let cool.

Makes around 2 dozen cookies, I think. I couldn't count because David hid them.

Logan's Chocolate Cars

THIS WAS THE TIME Williams and Sonoma came out with Cars cookie cutters, and another friend happened to request some airplane cut out cookies (and you know I'm a sucker for sending people cookies), so these had to be made. Sherry's little boy happened to be a complete Cars fanatic, and so is my son, so the cookie cutters were too tempting to resist. They got me. Now you can have your Lightning McQueen and eat him too. By the way, they make a cake pan as well. I'm just saying.

INGREDIENTS

1/2 cup butter or Earth Balance, softened

1/4 cup sugar

1/4 cup agave nectar (or maple syrup)

1 egg

1 tsp vanilla extract

3/4 cup all purpose flour

3/4 cup whole wheat flour

1/3 to 1/2 cup unsweetened cocoa powder (depending on how chocolatey you like your cookies. Yes, I put in the larger amount)

1/2 tsp baking powder

1/2 tsp baking soda

1/4 tsp salt

OPTIONAL GLAZE:

1 Tbsp butter or Earth Balance

1 cup confectioners sugar

1 tsp vanilla extract

2 to 3 Tbsp milk, soy milk, almond milk, or coconut milk

TO MAKE THE COOKIES

In a large mixing bowl, cream butter or Earth Balance, sugar, agave nectar, egg, and vanilla until thoroughly mixed and smooth. Combine dry ingredients in another bowl and stir. Add slowly to creamed mixture and mix until well blended. Form the dough into a ball and wrap in plastic wrap or wax paper. Chill in the refrigerator until firm, at least 1 hour or overnight—then let sit a few minutes at room temperature.

Preheat the oven to 325 degrees. Prepare two cookie sheets with liners.

Roll out on a lightly floured board until about 1/4 inch thickness. Cut out desired shapes and reroll until you have used all the dough. Bake on cookie sheets for 13 minutes or until the bottoms look dry and if you make a finger-print on the top, the cookie springs back. Cool slightly and then completely cool on wire racks.

If desired, mix glaze ingredients in a small bowl, adding more liquid if necessary to make a smooth glaze. Decorate cooled cookies as desired.

Makes 2 cookie sheets full, with maybe a spare car or 2.

Vanilla Brûlée Cookies

THIS WEEK WAS ANOTHER MAKE COOKIES FAST WEEK...We were on summer break from preschool and it was a bit crazy. Summer in the Seattle area is when all the relatives and friends come to visit in the hopes of getting a glimpse of summer sun, and avoiding all the heat back where they live. So we get pretty busy. Still, the cookie train must keep chugging, and these are a delicious twist on a sugar cookie and creme brûlée. The barley adds another dimension to the flavor. Plus, you get to use your kitchen torch if you have one! Five year old help not recommended with this one.

INGREDIENTS

1 1/4 cups all purpose flour

1 1/2 cups whole wheat flour

1/2 cup barley flour (or just add another 1/2 cup flour)

2 tsp baking powder

1 tsp salt

1 cup butter or Earth Balance, softened

1 cup sugar (I prefer unrefined especially in this recipe—the molasses flavor is great here)

Seeds scraped from two vanilla beans or 4 teaspoons of vanilla extract, or any combination

2 whole eggs

2 eggs, divided

TOPPING:

1 cup turbinado sugar

fire

TO MAKE THE DOUGH

Preheat the oven to 350 degrees. Line 2 cookie sheets with liners or parchment paper.

Combine the flour, baking powder, and salt in a medium bowl and set aside. In a large mixing bowl, cream the butter until smooth. Add the sugar, vanilla seeds or extract, eggs, and 2 egg yolks, and blend until fully combined. Add dry ingredients and mix until a nice dough forms.

Put half of the turbinado sugar in a bowl. Put the remaining egg whites in another small bowl and beat a little with a fork to blend.

Form tablespoon-sized (or larger) balls with your hands and then dip first in egg whites and then in sugar. Kind of like making sweet meatballs. Then place 2 inches apart on the cookie sheets and flatten with the bottom of a glass.

Bake until firm and lightly browned on the bottom, 15 to 20 minutes. Remove from oven and leave on the tray. Cool for about 5 minutes and then either sprinkle more sugar on each cookie or dip each cookie in sugar again. Use a new bowl because the old bowl had raw egg whites in it.

Here's the fun part: With a kitchen torch, melt the sugar on top of each cookie until it is caramelized and browned. It takes a little extra time, but provides a wonderful crunch and flavor. You could skip that step, though, if pressed for time, or if you don't have a kitchen torch, or if you are out of butane.

Makes about 26.

Grandma Bess' Mandelbrot

MY FATHER'S MOTHER, BESS, was famous for making these cookies, at least in our family. She would bake them and bring them in shoe boxes when she came to visit us, and we would literally try to hide the box from other visitors. If she came for a holiday, these would not be served at the table. More likely, one of the children would be caught in the corner of the kitchen trying to eat the entire box. Mandelbrot means "almond bread" but they are very much like biscotti, except they are "tri"scotti. This is her recipe with a few blasphemous changes (which I'm sure she would approve of...) Let me know if you can stop eating them.

INGREDIENTS

4 eggs

1 cup sugar

1 cup vegetable oil

2 Tbsp lemon juice

1 tsp vanilla

3/4 tsp lemon extract (or lemon oil)

1/2 tsp almond extract

3 to 4 cups all purpose flour

3 to 4 cups whole wheat flour

5 1/2 tsp baking powder

1/2 tsp salt

10 oz. toasted blanched slivered almonds (I buy the blanched slivered almonds and toast them)

TO MAKE THE COOKIES

Preheat the oven to 350 degrees. Line 2 cookie sheets with silicone liners or parchment paper.

Beat the eggs in a large mixing bowl until well blended, then add sugar, beating until light and fluffy. Add oil, lemon juice, vanilla, lemon and almond extracts and blend well. Add almonds. Starting with the smaller amount of flour, mix together flour, salt, and baking powder in another bowl. Mix into wet ingredients until dough is all combined and smooth (except for the lumpy almonds). If the dough is really sticky, add more flour until it is a consistency that can be rolled in your hands without losing half the dough between your fingers. These are the kind of cookies the weather might alter—I start with the smaller amount of flour, and add if necessary.

With oily hands roll dough between hands into 8 inch hot dog shapes (4 per sheet). Flatten the hot dogs to 3 inches across and 1/2 inch thick rectangles. Turn over so that each side gets smooth. Bake 40 minutes. Remove from the oven and immediately cut rectangles into half inch slices with a serrated knife and turn on their sides. Bake for another 10 minutes. Then, remove from the oven and flip slices to the other side.

The original recipe says "You will burn your fingers, but it is worth it." (I guess now I know why my grandmother seemed to have Teflon fingers.) Bake on the other side for 10 more minutes. Cool before packing. Lasts forever if no one eats them. Ha!

Makes 3–4 dozen depending on thickness.

Homemade Whoopie Pies

IT WAS TIME FOR CHOCOLATE AGAIN. You could tell, couldn't you? It was getting more difficult to come up with new cookie ideas, but come on, they're cookies! There must be a million flavors...that don't have any dairy in them. The jar of marshmallow fluff in my pantry inspired these.

INGREDIENTS

1 1/4 cups all purpose flour

3/4 cup whole wheat flour

3/4 cup unsweetened cocoa, preferably organic and fair trade

1/2 tsp baking soda

1/2 tsp salt

1/2 cup butter or Earth Balance

1/2 cup sugar or granulated evaporated cane juice

1 egg

1 cup milk, soy milk, almond milk or coconut milk I used coconut.

FILLING:

1 1/2 cups marshmallow fluff

TO MAKE THE COOKIES

Preheat the oven to 425 degrees. Line 2 baking sheets.

In a medium bowl, whisk together the dry ingredients. Cream the butter and sugar or substitutes in a large mixing bowl until smooth and creamy. Add the egg and beat until smooth. Then alternate adding the dry ingredients and the milk in several batches. Beat until all incorporated, chocolatey, and smooth.

Drop in rounded teaspoonfuls on the cookie sheets, 1 1/2 inches apart. Try to make the sizes approximately the same as they will be sandwiched together, and make an even number, unless of course you need a "tester."

Bake for 12 minutes, until they spring back to the touch and the bottoms are firm. Cool on a baking rack. Then spread the fluff (about a teaspoon) on one cookie and top with another. Repeat until all the cookies are done.

Place on wax paper and chill in the fridge to firm up, about one hour, if they will not be eaten immediately. Otherwise you will get crooked tower of Pisa cookies. If you are feeling very creative, you could just make a giant stack of these, alternating cookie and fluff. Maybe for a casual wedding or a birthday party? Time to stop now.

Makes 10 or so pies, depending on size.

Fruit Pie Cookies

THESE ARE LIKE ANOTHER VERSION of Hamantaschen, with a slightly different shape. The filling is interesting though, and not as sticky. They are great for lunchboxes. Use whatever jam/fruit combo makes you happy.

INGREDIENTS

1/2 cup butter or Earth Balance, softened

3 Tbsp brown sugar

1/2 tsp baking soda

1/2 tsp ground coriander

1/4 tsp salt

1 egg

1/2 cup honey

1 tsp vanilla extract

1 cup all purpose flour

1 1/2 cups whole wheat flour

FILLING:

1/2 cup apricot jam (or whichever fruit you happen to have)

1 1/2 cups mixed dried fruit (I used currants, cherries, and raisins)

1/3 cup chopped walnuts

TO MAKE THE COOKIES

In a large mixing bowl, cream the butter. Beat in the brown sugar, baking soda, coriander, and salt. Beat in the egg, honey, and vanilla. Beat in the flour until you have a good dough. Divide in half, flatten into discs, and chill through naptime or overnight.

In a small saucepan over low heat, melt the jam, stirring, for about 5 minutes. Stir in the dried fruits and nuts. Puree to a paste in the food processor if desired.

Preheat the oven to 375 degrees. Line 2 cookie sheets.

On your lightly floured board, roll one half of the dough to about 1/8 inch thickness. Cut into rounds using a drinking glass or round cookie cutter. I started with a smaller glass (about 2 1/2 inches) and then switched to about 3 inches. I actually liked the smaller cookies better, but they were harder to fill. Place the circles on the cookie sheets and spoon 1/2 teaspoon fruit/nut mixture on each. Fold the circles in half, sealing the edges with the tines of a fork. Repeat with the rest of the dough.

Bake until lightly browned, 10 minutes. Remove and cool on a rack.

Makes around 2 dozen.

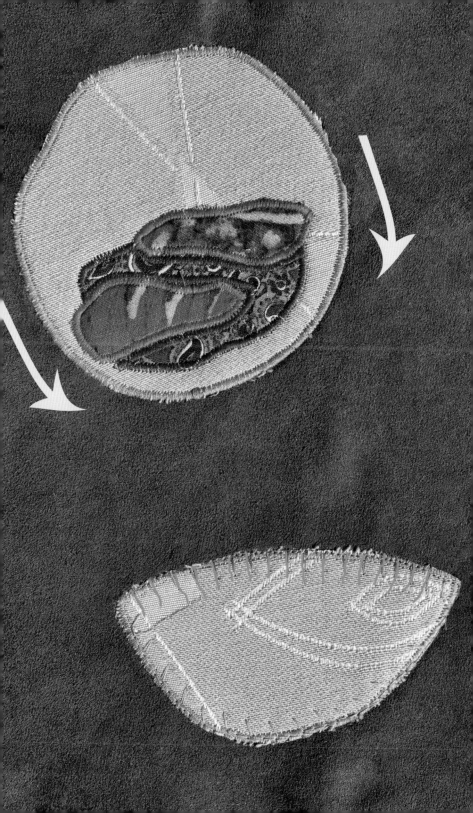

Oatmeal Snickerdoodles

OR HOW (NOT) TO BAKE WITH CHILDREN

THESE ARE A CHEWIER, crunchier, heartier version of a snickerdoodle, so if you like that, enjoy. There are some funny explanations on the internet for where the name "Snickerdoodle" originated; I will leave that to you to explore.

INGREDIENTS

3/4 cup butter or Earth Balance or other non-dairy margarine product, softened

3/4 cup sugar

2 tsp baking powder

1/2 tsp salt

1 tsp vanilla extract

1 Tbsp orange juice

2 eggs

1 1/3 cups steel cut oats, or rolled oats, ground in the food processor or not at all for more chewiness and less crunchiness

1 cup whole barley flour

3/4 cup whole wheat flour

TOPPING:

2 Tbsp turbinado sugar (extra crunchiness!)

2 tsp cinnamon

TO MAKE THE COOKIES

Wash everybody's hands. Cream the butter, sugar, baking powder, salt and vanilla in a large mixer bowl. Make sure to take turns adding ingredients! Beat in the orange juice, eggs, oats, barley flour, and whole wheat flour, scraping the bowl as needed, until combined. Easiest dough ever, right?

Remove, wrap or place in fridge container, and chill until firm enough to form balls, maybe 3 hours. Waiting is hard. Go swimming.

For topping, stir together sugar and cinnamon in a small bowl.

Preheat oven to 350 degrees. Line 2 cookie sheets.

Line up your two preschool aged children along the side of the counter. Make sure the children have washed their hands. With soap. Let the almost 5 year old take a small ball of dough, following you, and roll it in the cinnamon sugar. Place the ball on the cookie sheet. Give the 2 year old a small bit of dough. She will attempt to roll it, see her sticky hands, and slyly start eating small bits of the dough as her brother licks his sticky hands and is told to go wash his hands

92

again. As he leaves to wash his hands (screaming optional), remind her not to eat the dough, and do not give her any more dough. Continue to take teaspoons of dough from the bowl, roll them into balls and in the topping, and place them on the cookie sheets. When your son returns, let him continue to make and top balls of dough until your daughter has eaten all the dough in her hands and all the non-licked balls of dough are on the sheets, and the dough is all made.

Take a glass and start to flatten the balls of dough (leave about 2 inches between cookies). Tell your son that he can flatten with the glass ("I want to smash them!") if he can move the chair without disturbing his sister. Watch him pull the chair out from under her and start screaming that he still wants to do it even though she is screaming because she got her foot caught in the chair. Wait until everyone calms down and apologizes, and the 2 year old is busy with a toy. Then put your son back in the chair with the glass to smash the remaining cookies if possible. If not, he may need a time out. If the glass gets too sticky, coat it with some additional sugar.

Bake 15 minutes or until edges are brown. Remove the cookies from the sheets and let them cool on a rack.

Have a glass of wine or three.

Makes about two dozen, give or take lost dough.

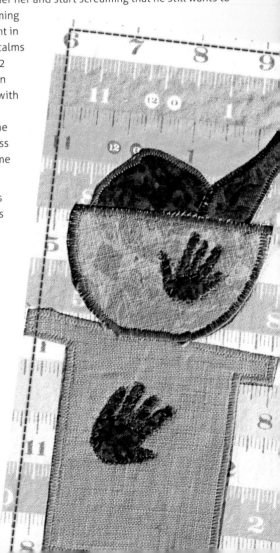

Mexican Wedding Cookies

I WAS ACTUALLY AVOIDING MAKING THESE because I am not a fan of Mexican Wedding Cookies. I always choke on the sugar, and it gets all over my hands, a problem I never have with chocolate. However, my husband David suggested them, although I never knew he was a fan either. Then I discovered they are made with pecans. Aha! Thus, the innocent suggestion. If you've read earlier recipes, you know that David is a huge fan of pecans. These are for you then, David.

INGREDIENTS

3/4 cup unsalted butter
(1 1/2 sticks) or Earth Balance (yes, it's a lot, well, they're Wedding Cookies, not for every day)

1/4 cup confectioner's sugar

2 1/2 tsp vanilla extract

1/2 tsp salt

1 cup finely chopped pecans

1 cup whole wheat flour

1 1/2 cups all purpose flour or whole wheat white or whole wheat pastry flour (or rice flour I guess, or almond flour!)

1/2 cup confectioners sugar
for coating

TO MAKE THE COOKIES

Preheat the oven to 350 degrees. Line cookie sheets and then oil liners with your fat of choice.

In a large mixing bowl, cream butter or substitute and sugar until light and fluffy, more than 5 minutes. Add vanilla, salt, and pecans and beat until all combined. Add in flour, and beat until well mixed.

Take teaspoons of dough and form into almond or ball shapes and place on cookie sheets 1 inch apart. Bake 12 minutes, or until bottoms are lightly browned.

Cool on sheets until cool enough to touch. You may have to burn yourself while testing, or you may choose to be virtuous (or efficient) and just clean the dishes while you wait.

When you can handle the cookies, throw a couple at a time into the confection-ers sugar and roll to coat. Put back on the cookie sheets and cool completely. Try to eat without choking on sugar dust.

Makes about 2 dozen.

Lemon Cornbread Bars

I WAS THINKING SUMMER MEANT LEMON, but then, our summer in the Northwest was kind of iffy this year, with regular showers through July. I couldn't complain though, because I'll always take that over the 100 degree temperatures the rest of the country was getting. Then Sara suggested lemon on my Facebook page as well, so I went with these. The first shortbread recipe I actually loved. It is a bit unorthodox though. As another friend (Laura) mentioned, while asking for the recipe, that they are a cross between shortbread and cornbread. A good midsummer afternoon snack.

INGREDIENTS

1 cup all purpose flour

1 cup whole wheat pastry flour

1 cup corn flour or finely ground cornmeal (you can use any grind I suppose, your texture will just vary a little)

1/2 tsp table salt

1 1/2 cups unsalted butter or Earth Balance, softened

1 cup confectioners sugar

1 Tbsp finely grated lemon zest

1/4 tsp lemon oil or 1/2 teaspoon lemon extract

1 tsp vanilla extract

TO MAKE THE COOKIES

Preheat the oven to 325 degrees. Grease (I spray with canola oil high heat spray) a 9 by 13 inch pan and then line with parchment paper and oil the paper. Leave edges overhanging the pan for easy removal.

In a medium bowl, combine the flour, cornmeal, and salt. In a large bowl, use an electric mixer to cream the butter or substitute with the sugar, lemon zest, extract or oil, and vanilla until smooth and creamy. Scrape the sides of the bowl and add the dry ingredients. Beat until smooth.

Spread the dough into the prepared pan, you may need to use your fingers to get it flat and even. Then take a dull knife and score the dough into bars all the way through.

Bake about 40 minutes or until the top is dry looking and the edges are starting to brown. Put the pan on a rack and cut the bars through before they cool and turn crumbly. Let cool completely.

Makes about 30, depending on size of cuts.

Whole Wheat Black and White Cookies

IF YOU GREW UP ANYWHERE NEAR NEW YORK, or anywhere near an authentic deli, or if you were a Seinfeld fan, you know about Black and White Cookies. They are like little cakes, frosted chocolate on half, and vanilla on the other half. They were originally made from left over cake batter. Some are huge; these are minis (so you can eat more than one). They are, I believe, my brother's favorite cookies. However, as he was living in the Philippines when I made these, I thought that was a bit far to send them. This version is a tad healthier and pareve as they are made with coconut milk. You can always switch them back to dairy if you like.

INGREDIENTS

1 1/4 cups sugar

1 cup butter or Earth Balance, softened

4 large eggs

1 1/2 cups coconut milk or soy milk or milk

1/2 tsp vanilla extract

1/4 tsp lemon oil or lemon extract or lemon juice

2 1/2 cups all purpose flour or cake flour

2 1/2 cups whole wheat flour

1 tsp baking powder

1/2 teaspoon salt

FROSTING:

4 cups confectioner's sugar

1 cup water

1/2 tsp vanilla

3 oz. unsweetened chocolate, chopped

TO MAKE THE COOKIES

Preheat the oven to 375 degrees. Line two cookie sheets with silicone liners or parchment paper.

In a large mixing bowl, cream the butter or substitute with the sugar until light and fluffy. Add eggs, one at a time, coconut milk, and extracts (or oils) and blend until smooth.

In another bowl, combine the flours, baking powder, and salt, and stir until mixed. Add the dry ingredients to the butter mixture in batches, mixing until it is all smooth. Using two teaspoons (one to scoop and one to scrape), place spoonfuls of dough on the cookie sheets 1 inch apart from each other. Bake for 20–22 minutes or until the bottoms are dry and starting to brown. Cool on a rack.

To make the frosting: Boil the water in a small pot. Place the confectioner's sugar in a microwave safe bowl and then add the vanilla and about 1/4 cup of the boiling water and stir until you get a spreadable frosting. If you need, you can add more water. Spread one half of each cookie with the frosting. You may want to spoon a little frosting over half and then use an offset spatula to spread it out. When you have finished frosting half of every cookie, add the chopped chocolate to the frosting and microwave the bowl for 30 seconds. Stir the frosting and heat for another 10 seconds. Stir until smooth. Keep heating and stirring for 10 seconds at a time until the chocolate is smooth enough to spread. Frost the other half of each cookie. *Voila!* You don't even need to find a decent deli!

Makes 24 little or 12 deli-sized cookies.

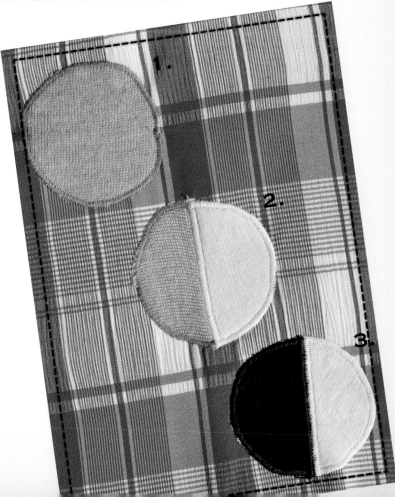

Alfajores

THESE DULCE DE LECHE SANDWICH COOKIES were recommended by my friend Ximena, who is from Argentina. I had never heard of them before, but once I started mentioning them to people who had actually been to Argentina, I started to hear raves. They didn't sound too hard (although there are at least 15 different types that are called Alfajores (al-fa-HOAR-eys) so I dug in with the kind I thought would mail the best (which left out the chocolate- or meringue-covered ones). As it was, I mailed a kit consisting of cookies, jars of filling, and coconut to roll it in. I hope it was a fun activity!

INGREDIENTS

2 cups whole wheat flour

2 cups white flour

2 tsp baking powder

1 tsp baking soda

1 tsp salt

1 cup butter or Earth Balance

3/4 cups sugar

1 tsp orange zest or 1/4 tsp orange oil

1 to 2 tsp cognac (if desired. Come on, you know you want it...)

2 eggs

1 to 2 jars dulce de leche (You can also make your own with sweetened condensed milk but you have to stand at the stove for a while) You can also try other fillings such as apricot or fig jam, which will make nice dairy free alternatives.

1/2 cup shredded coconut for coating (I used unsweetened as the dulce de leche is sweet enough already and you get more fresh coconut flavor—you can use the sweetened if that is your preference)

TO MAKE THE COOKIES

Preheat the oven to 350 degrees. Line 2 cookie sheets with silicone liners or parchment.

Mix the dry ingredients together in a medium bowl. In a large bowl, cream the butter or substitute with the sugar. Blend in the orange zest or oil and cognac. Add the eggs and continue blending. Slowly add the dry ingredients and blend until fully incorporated.

If desired, you can chill for a few minutes, but mine were a good consistency, so I went ahead and started baking them.

On a floured rolling surface, roll out the dough to 1/4 inch thickness and cut out circles of dough. I used a 2 1/2 inch glass, but you could go smaller. Place the circles on the cookie sheets 1 1/2 inches apart.

Bake for 12 minutes, until the cookies are firm but not browned. If they are slightly browned, don't worry. Cool on a rack.

To make the sandwiches, take two cookies at a time, spread a teaspoon of *dulce de leche* on one cookie and press the other on top so that some oozes out the sides. You may have to experiment with the correct amount. Roll the cookie in the shredded coconut so it sticks to the filling. Repeat until all cookies are sandwiched.

Makes around 2 dozen sandwiches.

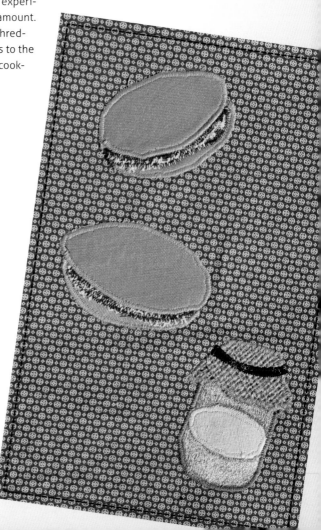

Blackberry Crumble Cookies

HERE IS ANOTHER REALLY VIVID INDICATION of the time of year through cookies. Here on Bainbridge Island we can pick blackberries almost anywhere for free in late August and September. They are an invasive (but often welcome) species that has run rampant here. When we first moved here, we joked that in a hundred years there would be nothing here but empty condos and blackberries. Well, the development seems to have slowed a little, but the blackberries are still going strong, and thus we get very creative about using them. These cookies are not attractive when the blackberries burst (and give them a grey color—as my son said, "Mommy, those don't look like cookies, but they smell good!"), but they taste delicious anyways.

INGREDIENTS

1/2 cup melted butter or Earth Balance

1/4 cup brown sugar

1/4 cup white refined or partially refined or whole cane sugar

2 eggs

2 tsp vanilla extract

1/4 tsp lemon oil or extract or juice

2 cups oats (I used steel cut because I was all out of old fashioned, and I toasted them. They make a crunchier cookie. You can use whatever oats you have on hand.)

1/2 cup toasted unsweetened shredded coconut (I toasted it for 5 minutes in the toaster oven)

1 1/2 cups whole wheat flour

1/2 tsp baking powder

1/2 tsp baking soda

a pinch of salt

1 to 1 1/2 cups fresh or frozen blackberries (or you can substitute blueberries)

TO MAKE THE COOKIES

Preheat the oven to 350 degrees. Line two baking sheets with silicone liners or parchment paper.

In a large mixing bowl, blend the butter and both kinds of sugar. Blend in the egg, vanilla, and lemon until all combined. Add the oats, coconut, flour, baking powder, baking soda, and salt and blend until you have a uniform dough. If it is too moist, add a little more flour. Gently fold in the blackberries by hand or by machine for brilliant purple cookies.

Don't forget this step as I almost did. If you do, then you will just have oatmeal-coconut cookies, which are good, but don't use up your blackberries!

Place spoonfuls of dough 2 inches apart on the cookie sheets. Bake 25 minutes (less if you made small cookies) or until bottoms are nicely browned. Cool on a rack.

Makes about 2 dozen.

Banana Split Cookies

YOU MAY HAVE READ EARLIER (week 20 to be exact, if you're reading this like a novel, which of course you probably aren't) that my husband David and I once raved over cookies like this at our favorite Philadelphia bakery. I finally decided to try them, and I got them pretty close, if I do say so myself. Of course, the bakery no longer exists, so you can't compare. Also, if you want a bit more history, I think there's a banana-chocolate thing going in my genes, because my father claims that his grandfather invented the chocolate covered frozen banana in his candy shop in Philadelphia. I can't prove it, but there it is. For a third useless fact, the banana split ice cream at Mora on Bainbridge Island is one of my favorite flavors in the world and if you ever come to Bainbridge, you have to go to that shop- it is incredible. OK, make the cookies already. I made 'em extra big, like the ones at the bakery, baby head sized cookies. You can make them smaller if you like.

INGREDIENTS

1 cup all-purpose flour

1 1/2 cups whole wheat flour

1/2 tsp baking soda

1 tsp baking powder

1/2 tsp salt

2/3 cup butter or Earth Balance, softened

1/2 cup brown sugar

1/4 cup maple syrup

2 eggs

1 1/2 tsp vanilla extract

1 1/2 to 2 cups mashed bananas
(I used 4 bananas, very ripe— lots of brown spots, the kind you would use for banana bread)

1 cup chocolate chips, melted

TO MAKE THE COOKIES

Preheat the oven to 400 degrees. Line two baking sheets with parchment paper or silicone liners if you have them. Line three sheets if you have them and plan on making the cookies really big, like I did.

In a large bowl, combine the flours, baking soda and powder, and the salt. Set aside. In a large mixing bowl, cream the butter or butter-like substance until smooth and creamy and then add the sugar and maple syrup, blend until smooth. Add the eggs, one at a time and blend some more. Add in the vanilla and the mashed bananas. You will have a gloppy batter. Mix in all the dry ingredients slowly, so it doesn't splatter all over the kitchen, until you have a smooth dough. Slowly add the melted chocolate and mix for about five seconds or until

you see chocolate swirls but the whole batter hasn't changed color. The swirl will give the cookies a marble effect. If you mix too long, they will just look like chocolate cookies that don't have enough chocolate in them.

Place the dough on the cookie sheets 2 inches apart by two tablespoonsful for large, bakery sized cookies, or teaspoons for a larger quantity of reasonable-portion-sized cookies. With the double tablespoon measure, I only got six to a sheet.

Bake for 18–22 minutes, only 16 minutes if you make the smaller version.

Cool on a rack. Enjoy with a tall glass of milk. Makes 10 extra big cookies.

105

Chocolate Caramel Sea Salt Cookies

MY FRIENDS AND I WERE DISCUSSING ICE CREAM and plastic packaging (of course, don't your friends discuss this?) on Facebook and we all agreed that this flavor combination was one of the best, and currently very fashionable to boot. How are those subjects related? —ice cream packed in non-recyclable packing. There's just something about the combination of salty and sweet. That has always been a favorite of mine since my grandparents served us pretzels and ice cream before bedtime. Do you see the recurrence of my grandparents in my sweet tooth history? Hmmm. Anyway, these were highly tested and retested to make sure they were an ideal combination. And they don't come in plastic. I think you'll like this combination of brownie-like cookie and crunchy caramel. Homemade caramel is an option. The smart option is to buy a jar. Really, I messed up the caramel far too many times.

INGREDIENTS

6 oz. bittersweet chocolate, chopped

7 Tbsp unsalted butter or Earth Balance

2 eggs

1 tsp vanilla

1 cup evaporated cane juice or sugar

2/3 cup all purpose flour

1/3 cup whole wheat pastry flour

1/4 tsp salt

1/4 cup cocoa

1 tsp baking powder

1/2 cup Turbinado sugar or sugar in the raw

CARAMEL:

1 cup confectioner's sugar

1/3 cup butter or Earth Balance

1/4 cup fleur de sel

TO MAKE THE COOKIES

Preheat the oven to 350 degrees. Line two cookie sheets with silicone mats or parchment paper.

In a medium bowl in the microwave, melt the chocolate. Melt in 15–30 second increments, stirring in between until it is all smooth. Set aside.

In a large mixing bowl, cream the butter, then beat in the eggs, vanilla, and sugars until they are thick and combined. Add the melted chocolate. In a separate bowl, mix all the dry ingredients together: flours, salt, cocoa, and baking powder. Slowly add the dry ingredients to the chocolate mixture and blend completely.

Place the Turbinado sugar in a bowl. With your hands, form Tablespoon sized balls of dough, roll them in the sugar, and place them 2 inches apart on the cookie sheet. Smash them flat. Wasn't that satisfying?

Bake for 12 minutes (do not overbake, they should be chewy!), remove and cool on trays. Not on a rack. Leaving them on the tray for a while will ensure maximum chewiness, good for these cookies.

While the cookies are baking, make the caramel. In a small saucepan over medium heat, blend the sugar and butter. Stir until the mixture boils,then keep stirring. In a few minutes, the sugar will melt and turn golden brown and thicken. It may be a thick gooey ball first, but it will get there. Keep stirring, then take off the stove. Or, you can just grab a jar of caramel sauce from the store. Much easier.

Drizzle the warm caramel over the cookies (about 1/4 teaspoon per cookie) and sprinkle with sea salt (a pinch).

It's hard to hold off, but these cookies are actually better a few hours to one day after they are out of the oven. So if you can wait, you'll get an even better cookie. Also great for do-ahead meals. — Enjoy!

Makes 2 dozenish.

Note: You can reuse leftover caramel by reheating on the stove, stirring constantly. I don't recommend attempting to reheat in the microwave.

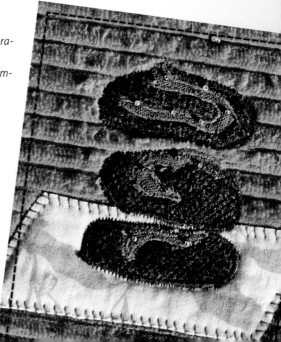

Date-Filled Pinwheel Cookies

AS I WAS FINISHING THE BOOK, I opened my *Joy of Cooking* one evening to check a recipe for dinner. On the inside cover, I found this inscription: "Happy Birthday 2003! You are a creative cook and could write your own cookbook—and maybe someday you will—with original illustrations! In the meantime—ENJOY—Love, Grandma and Granpop." Thanks for knowing me even more than I did Grandma. This recipe makes a lot of cookies and may be divided if you don't want 3 dozen or so.

INGREDIENTS

1 cup butter or Earth Balance

1/2 cup white sugar

1/2 cup brown sugar

1/4 cup maple syrup

3 eggs

1 tsp vanilla

2 cups all purpose flour

2 cups whole wheat pastry flour

1/2 tsp salt

1 tsp baking soda

3 tsp cinnamon

FILLING:

3 cups chopped dates
  (Sorry, but they taste good!)

2 Tbsp sugar

1 1/2 cups water, divided

TO MAKE THE COOKIES

Cream the butter, sugars, and syrup until smooth. Add the eggs, one at a time, and blend fully. Add the vanilla and then the rest of the ingredients and then blend until combined. You should get a thick, workable dough. Chill in the fridge while you make the filling.

Put the chopped dates, sugar, and one cup water in a small pan over medium heat on the stove. Boil, stirring constantly until the mixture thickens and darkens. Cool slightly, then put in a blender (a Vitamix if you are really lucky) with another 1/2 cup water. Blend until smooth and spreadable and remove from blender to bowl.

Divide the dough into three parts. Roll out each part (one at a time, silly) into a rectangle, about 1/4 inch thick. Spread with 1/3 of the filling, leaving a 3/4 inch edge for rolling. Roll up, jelly roll style, and seal the ends. Repeat with each section of dough and filling. Wrap the rolls with wax paper or plastic wrap. Chill in the fridge for two hours or until cold. If you do chill overnight, set out for a few minutes before cutting.

Preheat the oven to 400 degrees and line two cookie sheets with silicone liners or parchment paper. Slice the cookie rolls into 1/4 inch slices and place the slices on the sheets 1/2 inch apart. They can be pretty close together, they won't grow much. Bake for 10 minutes, remove and cool on racks.

Like I said, makes 3 dozen or so.

Index

Cookies By Category

QUICK DROP

ROLL IN SOMETHING AND BAKE OR VICE-VERSA

By Ingredient

DATE

GINGER

HONEY

LEMON

MAPLE